NAPOLEON

THE MAN

DMITRI MEREZHKOVSKY

Author of
"The Birth of the Gods," "Akhnaton, King of Egypt,"

TRANSLATED BY
CATHERINE ZVEGINTZOV

NEW YORK
E. P. DUTTON & CO., INC.

First Printing . . . *Oct., 1928*
Second Printing . . *Oct., 1928*

"The Fateful Executor of a Command Unknown"

PUSHKIN

NOTE

The translator wishes to express her deep gratitude to Mrs. Natalie Duddington, Miss Margot R. Adamson and Sir Bernard Pares for their generous help and advice, and also the two latter for their valuable contributions of most of the English versions from the Russian poets.

CONTENTS

NAPOLEON

CHAPTER I

THE JUDGES

THE object of every life story—"the life story of a hero" according to Plutarch, is to reveal the image of the man, to give a glimpse of his soul.

In this Napoleon was unlucky. It is not that little has been written about him; far from it—more indeed than about any other of our contemporaries. About forty thousand books have already been printed, and who knows how many more will be added? Nor are they useless. We know a great deal about his wars, policy, diplomacy, legislation and administration; about his ministers, marshals, brothers, sisters, wives, mistresses and even something about himself. Yet, strangely enough, the more we learn about him, the less we know him.

"This great man becomes more and more of an enigma," writes his contemporary, Stendhal.[1] "The history of Napoleon is the most obscure of all histories,"[2] says our contemporary Léon Bloy.

[1] Stendhal, *Vie de Napoléon.*
[2] Léon Bloy, *L'âme de Napoléon.*

Napoleon

Which means that for more than a hundred years the mystery of Napoleon has been growing greater. Yes, however strange it may seem, in spite of all his fame, Napoleon is unknown. Forty thousand volumes are as forty thousand tombstones, and beneath them lies the "Unknown Soldier." Perhaps the reason of this is that, as Heracletus has it, "Though one may go to a journey's end, the end of the soul can never be reached for it lies too deep." For the souls of those nearest to us and even our own are hidden from us.

Or, is it that his soul cannot be held captive in books? That it passes through them like water running through the fingers? Beneath the probing eye of history its mystery merely grows more profound like deep and transparent waters under the ray of a searchlight.

Yes, Napoleon's "mystery" is partly due to this, but not only to this. One cannot enter into another's soul, but one can either try to enter it or pass it by. It seems to me that we have passed by Napoleon's soul.

To know another's soul means to give it a valuation, to weigh it on the scales of one's own soul. And where is the soul that possesses scales for bearing the weight of Napoleon?

The Judges

"There is nothing which I can compare to the feelings experienced by me in the presence of this titanic being," says one of his contemporaries, who was not even a great admirer of his, rather the reverse.[3] Such was the impression created by him on all who approached him— friend and foe alike. Perhaps it was not even the greatness of his soul that caused it, but its undoubted magnitude which dwarfed the souls of all his fellow-men. He towered among us like Gulliver among the Lilliputians.

The tiny eyes of the Lilliputians could discern, as through a microscope, every cell in Gulliver's skin, but were unable to see his face. It appeared to them as a blurred and fearsome spot. With their little yard measure they were able to take exact measurements of his body, but to imagine or feel themselves as inhabiting within that body, was beyond them.

In like manner we are unable to feel ourselves as being within Napoleon's soul. Yet that is exactly what we ought to do if we are to know it. It is impossible to know another's soul unless one sees it from inside.

Only one man, perhaps, could as an equal pass judgment on Napoleon,—and that man was

[3] Thiébault, *Mémoires,* ed. 1862, iv.

Napoleon

Goethe. What Napoleon was in action, Goethe was in contemplation: both were the titans who had bridled chaos—the Revolution. That is why these two, like a pair of gigantic caryatids stand facing each other as it were at the threshold between the Middle Ages and our own times.

"The whole life of Goethe held no greater event than this super real of all beings called Napoleon," says Nietzsche.[4] "Napoleon is a compendium of the world." "His life was the stride of a demi-god. He was in a state of continual enlightenment. His destiny was more brilliant than any the world had seen before him or after him."[5] Such is Goethe's judgment—the judgment of an equal.

We, who are not his equals, fare even worse than did the Lilliputians with Gulliver. With us the difference in souls is not merely one in dimensions, growth or quantity, but in quality. The very nature of his soul differs from that of other people. That is why he inspired in all men such a mysterious, almost supernatural, awe, unlike anything known on earth. "The awe inspired by Napoleon," says Mme. de Staël, "is

[4] "Er hatte kein grössers Erlebniss als jenes ens realisimum." Nietzsche, Götter-Dämmerung, 1899.
[5] *Goethe's Conversations with Eckermann*, translated by Oxenford.

due to the particular effect of his personality on all who approached him. In the course of my life I came across men both worthy of respect and contemptible; but the impression produced on me by Napoleon was utterly unlike either." I soon realized that ordinary words fail to define his personality. He was neither good nor bad, neither cruel nor kind in the same sense as other men. A being so unique could neither inspire nor feel affection; he was either more or less than human; his appearance, his mind, his speech—all bore the stamp of some other nature." [6]

"He was a stranger in the world. All in him was mystery"—so did a seventeen-year-old Russian boy, Lermontov, fathom Napoleon whom he had never seen. "That most real of all creatures," who entered the world as no one else had done, the ruler of the universe is "a stranger in the world." He too might have said: "My kingdom is not of this world," though certainly not in the sense as these words had been uttered before.

He himself was conscious of that "other soul" in himself. "Among men I am always alone," was the life prophecy of the obscure seventeen-

[6] Mme. de Staël, *Considérations sur la Révolution Française,* Chaps. III and IV.

year-old lieutenant of artillery, Bonaparte.[7] And later at the summit of his glory: "I am like no one else; I make terms with no one." [8] Or referring to the statesman, *i.e.* himself: "he is always alone on one side, with the whole world on the other." [9] That "other soul" not only inspired awe and repelled, but also attracted men; it inspired them with love or hate in turn. "Everybody loved me and everybody hated."

God's messenger, the martyr for humanity, the new Prometheus crucified on the rock of St. Helena, a new Messiah; and an outlawed brigand, the Corsican cannibal, the Beast of the Apocalypse, the anti-Christ. Never, it would seem, have love and hate so striven over one man. Their conflicting rays playing about his face were too blinding for us to discern it. Did he discern it himself?

"Thousands of years will pass before circumstances such as mine will be repeated and produce another man like myself." [10] He says this without pride, or else his pride is so akin to humility that it is almost impossible to distinguish between the two.

[7] F. Masson, *Napoléon: Manuscrits inédits,* 1910.
[8] Rémusat, *Mémoires,* II. Engl. translation C. Hoey and J. Lillie.
[9] Rémusat, *Mémoires.*
[10] Lacour-Gayet, *Napoléon.*

The Judges

"Had I succeeded in accomplishing what I had conceived, I should have died crowned with the greatest glory ever attained by man. Even now, having failed, I shall nevertheless be looked upon as outstanding." [11] This is perhaps too humble an estimate. Here is another more humble still: "I shall soon be forgotten; historians will find little to say of me." [12] "Had a shot killed me in the Kremlin, I would have been as great as Alexander or Cæsar, for my work and my dynasty would have been established in France—whereas now I shall be almost nothing." [13] He says this at St. Helena, a living man from his grave; he speaks of himself calmly, dispassionately, as of a third person, as one living speaks of the dead, or perhaps, more serenely still—as one dead speaks of the living. He who is "a stranger in the world" is also a stranger to himself. He looks at himself from outside, for him his *ego* is no longer *I* but *he*.

It seems at times as if he knows himself as little as we know him. He knows merely that such as he are a heavy burden for the earth to bear. "When I die the whole world will say

[11] O'Meara, *Napoleon in Exile*, 1897, II.
[12] Gourgaud, *Journal inédit*, II.
[13] *Ibid*.

'ouf.' " [14] "Time will show whether it were not better for the peace of the world had I never lived." [15]

That is one aspect; here is another: "How many will hereafter regret my disasters and my fall!" [16] "You will weep tears of blood over me!" [17]

"In vera gloria?

Ai posteri ardua sentanzia." [18]

But posterity proved to be no better judge than his contemporaries.

"A portentous mixture of Quack and Prophet."—"'False as a bulletin' became a proverb in Napoleon's time."—"The compact, clear-seeing, decisive, Italian nature of him, strong, genuine . . . half-dissolved itself in a turbid atmosphere of French *fanfaronade*." "Having once parted with Reality, he tumbles helpless in Vacuity." "This poor Napoleon; our last Great Man!" Such is Carlyle's judgment in his famous book on "Heroes and Hero-Worship." If this judgment is correct, it is hard to understand how this "Quack who tumbles into Vacuity" could have found his place among

[14] Rémusat, *Mémoires.*
[15] Chuquet, *La Jeunesse de Napoléon,* II.
[16] Las Cases, *Memorial,* I. English version.
[17] Napoleon's speech in the 100 Days Chamber, 1815.
[18] Manzoni.

great men. However, Napoleon's image here outlined is so coarse, meagre and superficial as to be scarcely worth mentioning.

Taine is more forceful than Carlyle. His book on Napoleon appears to have made the last and lasting impression on the soul of his readers.[19] This impression produced on the heart and mind is due perhaps not so much to the talent and erudition of the writer as to his being in harmony with the spirit of the times: Taine but gave utterance about Napoleon to what had been in everyone's mind.

"Measureless in all things, and so the more strange, he not only exceeded all limits, but also could be constrained within no boundaries. In his temperament, instincts, ability, imagination, passions, morality, he seemed cast in a mould and of a metal which differed from those of his contemporaries.

"Since the time of Cæsar the world has never seen such a genius in the width and depth of his conceptions, in the heroic force of spirit, intellect and will."

Such is the beginning. Let us now listen to the end: "The Napoleonic policy is a labour of egoism which genius serves. His whole pan-Euro-

[19] Taine, *Les Origines de la France Contemporaine,* IX. *Le Régime Moderne,* Chap. I.

pean edifice, even as the French are, was ruined by the egoism which dominated it."

Among men Napoleon is "a magnificent beast of prey, let loose among a peacefully grazing herd." When in 1813 in Dresden he says to Metternich that: "a man such as I snaps his fingers on the lives of a million men," he shows the boundlessness and ferocity of his ambition. "Without doubt, it is impossible to live with a character such as his: his genius is too great and too harmful, and its harm increases with its greatness." "Such is this egoism, grown to monstrous size and rearing in human society a gigantic ego which gradually widens the grasp of its avid tentacles, that every resistance offends it, every liberty hampers, and in the boundless sphere of its dominion it tolerates no life which is not an attribute or instrument of its own."

In other words, a spider holding the world like a fly in its claws and sucking its life blood; or an infernal machine invented by the devil to destroy the universe; or finally the Beast of the Apocalypse emerging from the pit; "Napoleon —Apollyon, the Destroyer," such was the interpretation given to his name by the contemporary expounders of the Apocalypse.

"Make haste, my mother, come and see the

savage, the man-tiger . . . the fruit of your womb," he laughingly would say, on reading such libels.[20]

When in 1814 after his first abdication he was being conveyed to the island of Elba by the commissioners of the Allies, his effigy was hung on a gallows by the royalists of the little town of Aurgonne in Provence amid shouts of "down with the Corsican! down with the brigand!" of the mob, While the mayor of Aurgonne made a speech: "I will hang him with my own hands and avenge myself for what happened before." What did happen "before" was that after Bonaparte's return from Egypt that same mayor had made a welcome speech to the conqueror on his bended knees.[21]

Taine's attitude is somewhat similar: at the beginning of his book he worships the hero, whose effigy he hangs at its close. "The heart is less likely to become hardened by the most cruel facts than by abstractions." "Soldiers are better than lawyers"; said Napoleon as if he foresaw the treatment he was to receive at the hands of "lawyer-idealists." [22]

That Taine's book remained unanswered is a

[20] *Memorial*, III, English version.
[21] Bourrienne, *Mémoires*. V.
[22] J. Bertaut, Napoléon Bonaparte, *Virilités*.

sign of the times. Arthur Lévy's impotent
though conscientious effort to prove Napoleon
to be nothing more than "a good bourgeois to
the backbone" cannot even be looked upon as an
answer.[23]

Another sign of the times: East and West
agree in their verdict on Napoleon: the atheist
Taine was in accord with the believer Leo Tolstoy. The judgment pronounced on Napoleon by
the drunken servant Lavrushka in "War and
Peace" is that of Tolstoy himself. Napoleon
commits only "fortunate crimes." He is "a brilliant and conceited mediocrity."—"Childish te-
merity and self-assuredness bring him extraordinary fame." He shows "unparalleled stupidity
and baseness"; "that final degree of baseness
which every child is taught to be ashamed of." [24]

The Russian prophet remained as unanswered
as did the European savant. The human herd
rushed greedily at the bait provided by their
shepherds. "The mob in its baseness rejoices in
the humiliation of the exalted, the weakness of
the strong: 'he is as small as we are, he is as
vile as we!' You lie, wretches:—he may be small

---

[23] Arthur Lévy, *Napoléon Intime*.
[24] L. Tolstoy, Article on the Campaign of 1812. Suppl. to *War and Peace*.

and vile; yet not as you are—but otherwise!"
(Pushkin).

In complete contrast to Taine and L. Tolstoy
stands Léon Bloy. His book "The Soul of Napoleon," a book weird, incoherent, boundless, at
times almost insane but imbued with profound
genius, is one of the most remarkable works on
Napoleon.[25]

Its novelty and penetration lie in that in it a
legend, or rather what seems to be a legend but
is actually a religious experience, both individual and national, is made by the author to serve
as a method of historical research. The author
knew, as did the initiated in the Eleusinian mysteries, that a myth is not an invented fable, but
prophetic symbolism in forecasted shadow of a
hidden truth, a pall covering the mystery, which
cannot be fathomed unless that pall is lifted.
The way to the hero's soul lies through one's
own and through the nation's soul; through the
Napoleonic legend—to the Napoleonic mystery
—such is the course followed by Bloy.

"Napoleon cannot be explained; he is the most
inscrutable of men, because he is primarily and
above all the prototype of Him Who must come
and Who, perhaps, is not far distant; he is the

[25] Léon Bloy, *L'âme de Napoléon,* 1920.

prototype and forerunner, closely akin to us."
"Who among us, Frenchmen or even foreigners,
living at the end of the 19th century but has felt
the illimitable sadness of the consummation of
this incomparable Epic? Who possessed with
but an atom of a soul but was not overwhelmed
by the thought of the verily too sudden down-
fall of the great Empire and its Leader? Who
was not oppressed by the remembrance that but
yesterday, so it seemed, men were on the highest
pinnacle possible to humanity, because of the
mere presence of this Beloved, Miraculous and
Terrible Being, the like of whom had never before been seen in the world; and could, like the
first human beings in paradise deem themselves
lords of all God's creation, and now immediately
after must again be cast back into the age-long
mud of the Bourbons." [26] Paradise lost and regained—this is the pall of the Napoleonic legend covering the Napoleonic mystery; it is here
that the soul of the people has come in contact
with the soul of the hero.

"The ravings of a lunatic or a cheap lithograph," Taine might perhaps have said about
Bloy's book, and would have been mistaken. Was
not the "psychology of the masses" between 1793

[26] Léon Bloy, *L'âme de Napoléon*, 9–10.

and 1815 like "the ravings of a lunatic," and did
not a "cheap lithograph" furnish a precious doc-
ument to the historian? Bloy is precious just because within his own soul he preserves the Napoleonic "psychology of the masses," revives the
Napoleonic legend. When he speaks of "his
Emperor" tears glisten in his eyes as they glis-
tened in the eyes of the old be-whiskered grenadiers of the Grande Armée. He is precious, as a
proof that Napoleon still lives in the soul of
Frenchmen, in the soul of France; perhaps he
is more alive even now than ever before; from
beneath forty thousand volumes—tombstones—
still rises the Unknown Soldier.

Not only Frenchmen—all Europeans must
know this: because they all may need a Hero:
"you will weep tears of blood over me." Bloy
calls himself a "good Catholic," though in the
eyes of good Catholics he is a rank heretic.
There is no doubt, however, of his being a Christian, or at least of wanting to be one. But even
a Christian is sometimes at a loss to determine
whether his utterances are prayers or blasphe-
mies. In any case it is too bold and hasty an assertion that Napoleon is "the forerunner of Him
Who must come." Who actually must come remains obscure, but apparently it is the Paraclete,

the new Adam, Who will restore paradise to the old Adam—mankind. His solution: "I cannot picture to myself paradise without my Emperor" is too painless and simple.[27] Napoleon in paradise side by side with Joan of Arc—that is something which requires proof not only to "good Catholics." How to unite Joan of Arc with Napoleon in paradise, that is the question.

It is equally difficult to determine whether Bloy prays or blasphemes when he says: "God gazed into the blood-stained mirror of war, and it reflected the image of Napoleon. God loves him as His own image. He loves this Aggressor as well as the meekest of His Apostles, Martyrs and Confessors." [28]

Yes, perhaps that is blasphemy, but before deciding let us recall the words: "I have trodden the wine press alone; and of the people there was none with me: for I will tread them in mine anger, and trample them in my fury; and their blood shall be sprinkled upon my garments, and I will stain all my raiment" (Isaiah 63: 3).

That is why even the meekest of the Apostles knows that "it is a fearful thing to fall into the hands of the living God." Had we not for-

[27] Léon Bloy, *L'âme de Napoléon.*
[28] *Ibid.*

18

gotten this, then perhaps in our own times the face of God would not have cast in the "blood-stained mirror of war" a reflection more terrible than ever before.

In any case it is impossible, as did Taine, to hold Napoleon alone responsible for the 2,000,000 lives lost in his wars.[29] The war waged by Europe against France was a legacy inherited by him from the Revolution, and he was power-less to put an end to it even had he wanted to. He was right in saying: "My defeat at Marengo would not have altered the events of 1814 and 1815."[30] He healed not only France but perhaps the whole of Europe from the scourge of civil war, and we now know by experience how far more terrible than a foreign is a civil war. The Napoleonic wars are child's play in comparison with the Great War and the Russian civil war with their 15,000,000 killed, 30,000,000 dead from epidemics and 5,000,000 from starvation. And all this happened notwithstanding or per-haps even because of the absence of a Napo-leon in our midst.

However that may be, Bloy is certainly right in one respect: the history of Napoleon will

---

[29] Léon Bloy, *L'âme de Napoléon.*
[30] *Memorial,* III.

either remain forever "the most obscure of all
histories," or will be illumined by the light of
Christianity, because the Napoleonic legend is
still almost a Christian mystery in the soul of
the people, and there is no other way to the
hero's soul than through the soul of the nation.
This means that the final judgment on Napoleon
will be pronounced not by "lawyers and ideologues," the authors of forty thousand volumes,
not by those who talk, but by those who are
silent—the people.

What do the people think of Napoleon? This
is hard to learn, not merely because the people
are silent, but also because their thoughts are
not our thoughts.

To the people Napoleon was simply "The
Man," *l'Homme,* as if by this they meant that
he more than any other had the fullness of the
measure of mankind. He was also the "Little
Corporal," as a proof that he was one with the
simple folk. And the hero agreed to this. "I
had the reputation of being a monster only in
your salons, among officers and perhaps generals,
but never among the men. With their instinct of
truth and sympathy they knew that I was their
protector." [31] "Popular fibre responds to mine;

[31] *Memorial,* I.

The Judges

I am come from the ranks of the people, and my voice has influence over them. Observe these conscripts, these sons of peasants: I did not flatter them, I treated them with severity . . . they did not the less shout: 'The Emperor for ever!' It is because between them and me there is an identity of nature." [32]

Yes, men followed him, as for the last two thousand years no man has been followed. They followed him across seas and rivers, over mountains and plains, from the Pyramids to Moscow; they would have followed him further still, to the confines of the earth had he but led them. They followed him through untold hardships, suffering, thirst, famine, scorching heat, disease, wounds, death itself—and were happy. . . . And he knew this: "Great was my material power, but my spiritual power was infinitely greater; it bordered on magic!" [33]

When in the thick of the battle he cried: "Soldiers, I want your lives, you must sacrifice them for me," the men knew that they *must.* "None did the soldiers serve as loyally as they served me. With the last drop of blood oozing from their veins they cried: *'Vive l'Empereur!'* " [34]

[32] *Memorial,* II.   [33] *Memorial,* III.   [34] O'Meara, I.

Napoleon

Within living memory no catastrophe was equal in horror to the destruction in the Russian campaign in 1812 of the Great Army of six hundred thousand strong men. Napoleon knew, as did all his troops, that neither the burning of Moscow, nor the cold, nor the betrayal of the Allies were to blame for this catastrophe; only he alone. Did the army mutiny or murmur? No. Only the old whiskered grenadiers grumbled softly, still plodding on, only now no longer following him but abreast, because he too plodded through the snow, stick in hand, in their midst. "Only the shadow of the Great Army reached the Beresina; but still he was to them what hope is to the human heart." Walking alongside of the soldiers he had nothing to fear from them, he talked to them kindly and they responded in the same strain. "They would sooner turn their arms against themselves than against him." "They fell and died at his feet; yet even in their dying delirium they did not abuse against him but prayed for him." [35]

A shudder of horror passed over France when the 29th bulletin announcing the destruction of the Great Army was received. It ended with the words: "His Majesty's health has never been

[35] Ségur, *Hist. and Mém.* ed. 1873, vol. V.

better." "Families, dry your tears: Napoleon is in good health!" was Chateaubriand's bitter comment.[36] But the simple folk wept when on his return to Paris Napoleon announced a fresh mobilization and told them: "You chose me, I am your handiwork, you have to defend me!" [37] Three-hundred thousand men perished in the campaign of 1812; in the new conscription 180,-000 were called to the colours. They were all very young; the older ones had been drafted long ago. "These brave lads are thirsting for glory; they look neither to right nor left, but always forward," was Marshal Ney's glowing tribute. Napoleon too admired them: "They simply spurt courage!" [38]

When these too were slaughtered at Leipzig, fresh recruits had to be called up, mere smooth-cheeked boys, so like girls—they were nick-named "Marie-Louises." Many of them did not know how to load a musket. Yet after a few days' campaign they emulated the old veterans of '96, the conquerors of the world.

The words of a contemporary on Napoleon's triumphant march from Elba to Paris could well be applied to his whole life: "The march

[36] Lacour-Gayet. *Napoléon.*
[37] *Ibid.*
[38] *Ibid.*

of the human multitudes following him was like the fiery trail of a meteor on a dark night." [39]

The people remained faithful to the end, and would have followed him even after Waterloo. On the way from Malmaison to Rochefort— to St. Helena—crowds ran after him shouting amid their sobs: *"Vive l'Empereur! Stay, stay with us!"* [40]

Deputies, ministers, marshals, brothers, sisters, wives, mistresses—all betrayed him, only the people remained faithful. The more exalted their position, the nearer they are to him, the less they love and understand him; and the more lowly their station, the further they are removed from him—the greater their love and clearer their insight. "Because Thou hast hid these things from these wise and prudent and hast revealed them unto babes."

During the White Terror of 1815 in Marseilles the Royalists tried to compel an old Egyptian Negress to shout *"Vive le Roi!"* She refused and shouted: *"Vive l'Empereur!"* She was knocked down by a bayonet thrust in the stomach, but endeavouring to rise and holding her intestines in her hands shouted once more:

[39] Thiébault, V.
[40] Houssaye, *1815,* III.

The Judges

"Vive l'Empereur!" They hurled her into the waters of the old port; she gathered all her strength, and rose once more to the surface and sank with a last cry of *"Vive l'Empereur!"* [41]

Yes, for two thousand years no one had inspired mankind with such love and such a readiness to die for him.

It is terrible to hear him say: "Such a man as I does not care a snap for the lives of a million men!" Still more terrible perhaps is the reply of millions of men: "We do not care a snap for our lives in the cause of a man like you!"

What is it they love in him? What do they die for? for their Country, for the Man, the Brother? Yes, but also for something else greater than these. It seems the poet rightly guessed what the Old Guard died for at Waterloo:

> Comprenant qu'ils allaient mourir dans cette fête,
> Saluerent *leur dieu* debout dans la tempête. [42]

Though had anyone told the two grenadiers who shielded him with their bodies from an explosion at St. Jean d'Acre, that he was their god, they would have been puzzled, or might have laughed even, for like good old *sans culottes* they did not believe in any God. [43]

[41] Houssaye, *1815*, III.
[42] Victor Hugo, *Châtiments*.
[43] *Memorial*, I.

Napoleon

On the eve of Austerlitz as the Emperor was making a tour of inspection, the soldiers suddenly remembered that this was the first anniversary of his coronation. Quickly they lighted whisps of straw and dry twigs from the campfires which they fixed to the bayonets and saluted the Emperor with eighty thousand torches.[44]

He knew already, and through him by some oracular premonition—the Napoleonic genius —the whole army knew, that to-morrow's "sun of Austerlitz" would rise radiant in the heavens. It was thus mentioned in the bulletin: *le soleil se leva radieux.*" ("The sun rose radiant.") But what sun it was that they worshipped at this fiery vigil, the men ignored. Had they lived between the second and third centuries A. D. instead of the nineteenth they would have known: the god Mithras, the Invincible Sun—*Sol Invictus.*

To grasp this that poor "ideologue" Nietzsche had to become insane: "Napoleon is the last incarnation of Apollo, the sun-god." The sage Goethe seemed to know this too, when he said: "He was in a state of continual enlightenment. His destiny was the most brilliant that

[44] Ségur, II.

the world had ever seen, so suffused was it with sunlight."

"Are you cold, *mon ami?*" Napoleon asked an old grenadier trudging beside him at Beresina in fifty degrees of frost. "No, Sire, when I look at you I feel warm," he replied.[45]

A like answer might have been given by an ancient Egyptian to his Pharaoh, the sun-god: "Verily, thou proceedeth from the Sun, as a child from its mother's womb." [46] The Sun-myth of the suffering god-man—Osiris, Thammuz, Adonis, Attis, Mithras, that immemorially ancient myth of the whole mankind—is but a pall concealing the mystery of Christianity.

The sunrise is bright, but the sunset is steeped in the blood of the immolated victim; the sun of Austerlitz sets at St. Helena. St. Helena is more sublime than the whole of Napoleon's life; his victories, his glory and greatness all led to it; his life cannot be understood, or visualized otherwise than through it.

Does he pray or blaspheme, when at St. Helena he says: "Jesus Christ would not be

[45] Lacour-Gayet.
[46] Hymn to the Pharaoh Akhnaton, on the tomb of Tel-el-Amarna, 1350 B.C.

God if He had not died on the Cross"?[47] How
could such words fall from the same lips which
said: "A man like myself does not care a snap
for the lives of a million men"? Or does he not
realize the burden of what he says? Granted—
but still these are not mere empty words, but
perhaps the most weighty, momentous, and decisive saying on which his whole destiny depended and one which ruled his whole destiny.

Let him imagine that St. Helena is not a sacrifice, but a punishment. To interpret and perhaps to justify him is after all to interpret St.
Helena, to demonstrate why it was not an execution but a sacrifice, not a doom but salvation.
Nothing of this kind could have happened to
Alexander or Cæsar, while without it Napoleon
could never have become the hero of Christian
France,—yes, a Christian in spite of everything,
and of Christian mankind.

Thus too did the people interpret him. Herein
is the meaning that the Napoleonic legend is
laid as a pall on the mystery of Christianity. "I
cannot picture paradise without my Emperor,"
—the people too might have said it.

One day, when Napoleon was in exile on
Elba. three soldiers entered a tavern in Paris

and ordered four glasses. "But there are only three of you," said the astonished host. "Never mind, do as you're told, the fourth will turn up!" The fourth—Napoleon.

When long ago two of the faithful used to meet in the street, one would ask: "Dost thou believe in Jesus Christ?" And the other replied: "I believe in Him and His resurrection!" [48]

On his return to Paris from Elba on the 20th March, 1815, Napoleon was borne into the palace of the Tuileries shoulder high by the crowd. "Those who carried him were frantic, beside themselves with joy, and thousands of others deemed themselves happy to be able to kiss or even touch the hem of his garments." "Methought I was present at Christ's resurrection." [49]

Towards France there journeyed two grenadiers
Who had long been prisoners in Russia. . . .

The same perhaps who shielded him from an explosion at St. Jean d'Acre with their bodies. One of them bids the other bury him in a foreign land:

[48] Lacour-Gayet.
[49] Thiébault, V.

Napoleon

So, listening in silence, evermore
In my grave like a sentry staying,
I will wait till I hear the cannon's roar,
And the charging coursers neighing.

I shall know that the Emperor rides o'er my grave,
While swords clash on swords affrighted,
And seizing my arms I will rise from my grave,
That the Emperor, God bless him! be righted.[50]

This means: Napoleon will rise again and raise the dead.

"When I was a child I knew old veterans who could not distinguish him (Napoleon) from the Son of God," writes Bloy.[51]

If that is blasphemy, Napoleon himself is guiltless of it. "Pray not to compare me with God. Such expressions when applied to me are so strange and irreverent that I wish to believe you did not think of what you were writing," is Napoleon's rebuke to that imprudent flatterer, the Minister of Marine, Decrès.[52]

He was not an atheist, but neither was he a Christian. In his testament he writes: "I die in the Roman apostolical religion, in the bosom of which I was born." [53] Though he was born and died in the Christian religion, he lived outside

[50] Heine, *Two Grenadiers* (translated by T. Brooksbank).
[51] Bloy.
[52] Arthur Lévy.
[53] *Memorial,* IV.

it, in fact as if Christianity had never existed at all. "I prefer Islam, at least it is not as absurd as our religion." [54] This was also spoken at St. Helena, and these, too, are not mere empty words.

Goethe's assertion that Napoleon is "a compendium of the universe" is not quite correct. Nay, not of the whole universe, but only of half of it—that half which we term "pagan"; the other one, which we call "Christian" is shut off from Napoleon. It is full of darkness to him, just as Hades, the realm of shadows, the nocturnal hemisphere of the heavens meant darkness to the ancients. That both hemispheres, the diurnal and nocturnal, meet is unknown to him.

To treat Napoleon as the forerunner of the Coming Christ is as absurd and impious as to see in him the precursor of the anti-Christ. Herein lies the tragedy of his life, and not only his but ours too—for is he not our last hero— that he himself knows not whose forerunner he is. In this, the crux, he is neither yea nor nay, but a question which has no answer.

"Oh, well, a man like myself is always either a god or a devil," [55] This with a laugh, as men

54 Gourgaud, II.
55 O'Meara, II.

will sometimes laugh when afraid. For indeed is it not fearful for him and for us too—not to know whose envoy—God's or Satan's—is this last hero of Christian mankind.

"Napolcon is a *daimoniac being,*" says Goethe using the word *daimon* in its antique pagan sense: neither god nor devil but someone betwixt the two.

A hero of the West, Napoleon is himself akin to the sunset, the eventide of the world. Because of this he remains forever the Mysterious and Unknown.

Of all that could be said of him, Pushkin's epitome seems to be the most profound:

"The Fateful Executor of a Command Unknown."

That is why no judgment passed by man can touch him.

CHAPTER II

THE BUILDER OF CHAOS

WHAT is the secret of Napoleon's power to attract men? Why was the tumultuous rush of human multitudes in his wake like "the fiery trail of a meteor on a dark night?"

Comte de Ségur, who took part in the Russian campaign, thus describes the entry of Murat's cavalry on the 14th September 1812, into Moscow, as yet untouched by fire, but already deserted and menacingly still:

"Seized with a secret tremor, the riders listened to the clatter of their horses hoofs"— the only sound amid the stillness of the vast depopulated city, where—"wondering, they heard no one but themselves in the midst of a multitude of houses." [1]

This feeling of "wonder," this "secret tremor" is the same apocalyptic strain which runs throughout the whole Napoleonic mystery. It originated earlier still with the Revolution when at times it reached such a pitch

[1] Ségur, V.

33

that it is almost akin to the early Christian eschatology, the premonition of the world's approaching end: "The end of all things is at hand. There will be a new heaven and a new earth." In this feeling are united the beginning and the end of Time. Immemorial antiquity: "forty centuries look down on you from the Pyramids," and boundless novelty, an unheard of, unique compendium of sensations: never has this been seen by mortal eyes nor will be seen again. In ecstatic awe, as before the Second Coming of Christ, the frenzied cry of the visionaries: *"Maran atha!"* ("The Lord cometh!")

"We had outstripped all the heroes of antiquity," says Ségur, "we had drunk our fill of glory. Then suddenly sadness would overcome us: was it that we were exhausted by the volume of all our emotions, or was it due to our sense of utter loneliness on the dizzy heights we had scaled and whence we could contemplate the boundless spaces stretching before us?"

The same eschatology is found in Léon Bloy's book: "when men had attained the highest pinnacle possible to humanity, because of the mere presence of this Beloved, Miraculous and Terrible Being, the like of whom had never been seen in the world—and so they could, like the first humans in paradise deem themselves lords of all God's creation."

The ancient dream of paradise lost, of God's kingdom on earth as in heaven, together with the new vision of a human kingdom of Liberty, Equality and Fraternity drew man towards Napoleon.

This signifies that the soul of Napoleon is the soul of Revolution. He is the lightning in that storm, the sea serpent cast up from that deep.

He is the nursling of the Revolution as Romulus was that of the she-wolf. He might curse it, or try to kill it—yet always he would return to it and cling to its iron nipples: the blood flowing in his veins was the wolf's milk of the Revolution.

He is the Revolution incarnate: "I am the French Revolution," he said after the execution of the Duc d'Enghien, one of the most terrible and cruel, though not insane, of his acts: that murder consolidated his link with the regicides of 1793, and with the soul of the Revolution, the Terror. The moat of the Vincennes fortress, where the innocent descendant of the Bourbons met his death, is the Rubicon between the old order and the new—the cutting of the navel-string joining the new-born Cæsar with the ancient Royalty. The body of the Duc d'Enghien served as the first step for Bonaparte's assent to the imperial throne; the blood of Enghien was his imperial purple.

"Only by weakening every other power shall I consolidate my own," he said, speaking at the Council of State on his coronation.[2] And in reply to Chateaubriand's ambiguous speech at the Académie concerning the writer Joseph Chénier, a regicide of '93: "How dares the Académie mention regicides, when I, a crowned monarch, who ought to hate them even more, dine with them and sit at the Council table beside Cambacérès?" (a former member of the Convention and a regicide, now State Chancellor).[3]

Truly, this Cæsar was anointed not by the myrrh for the most holy Ampulla but by the revolutionary will of the people. "I have not usurped the crown; I have raised it out of the mire; the people placed it on my head; let their acts be respected.[4]

"I am the French Revolution," says he at the beginning of the Empire; and at the end: "The Empire is the Revolution."[5]

[2] Lacour-Gayet.
[3] *Ibid.*
[4] *Memorial*, I.
[5] Houssaye, *1815*, I.

The Builder of Chaos

The Revolution is the soul of the Empire, its driving force, as the soul is the driving force of the body. Let cracks but appear in the structure of the Empire, and the fiery lava of Revolution gushes forth through the fissures.

"It's time to put on the riding boots of '93 again," says Napoleon at the time of the Allied offensive in 1814.[6] And again in 1815 on the eve of Waterloo: "Emperor, Consul, soldier—I hold everything from the people. . . . My will is the will of the people; my rights are their rights."[7] And after Waterloo before his departure for Rochefort—on the last journey to St. Helena: "The European powers are waging war not against me, but against the Revolution."[8]

That is the reason why such an honest old Jacobin as Carnot, a member of the *Comité du Salut Public,* a Don Quixote and philanthropist of '93, remains loyal to him to the end. While "France's honour and happiness do not allow one to doubt that Napoleon's cause is the cause of the Revolution," is another Jacobin's explanation of his loyalty.[9]

[6] Lacour-Gayet.
[7] Houssaye, *1815,* I.
[8] Houssaye, III.
[9] Thibaudeau, *Mémoires,* 1913.

Napoleon

"Don't let him join forces with the Jacobins!" exclaimed the Emperor Alexander I repeatedly, a prey to superstitious dread, when the news of Napoleon's escape from Elba reached the Congress in Vienna. Alexander alone, it seems, realized the danger of Napoleon once more becoming what he had been already—Revolution incarnate, a "Robespierre on horseback."

None knew better than Napoleon that hellish horror—the Medusa-like face of the Revolution, which turned to stone all living. "A revolution is one of the greatest evils with which Heaven visits mankind." [10] The revolutionary "rabble," the *"vile canaille"* is repugnant to him both in the physical and metaphysical sense. As he stands in the Place du Carrousel and watches the mob storm the Tuileries on the 10th August, 1792, his face blanches and he mutters through his teeth: *Che coglione!* (what rabble!) How could they let them get in? Why don't they use grape-shot, if a few hundred were shot down, the others would run away!" [11]

"He knows no human fear; yet he grows pale when he hears of the atrocities which a people in revolt becomes capable of. If, as he passes through the streets of Paris, a workman falls on

[10] *Memorial*, III.
[11] Lévy.

38

his knees before him imploring some favour, his first impulse is to recoil.[12]

"He was a bad man, an evil man!"—he says of Rousseau standing over his grave. "Without him there would have been no French Revolution. . . . It is true that I, too, would not have existed. . . . Perhaps that would have been better for the happiness of France." [13] "Your Rousseau is a madman; it is he who has brought us to this." [14] "Time will show whether it would not have been better for the peace of the world if neither Rousseau nor I had lived.[15]

Yet he knows that the Revolution had to be, that it is ruled by the same destiny which rules him. "I think our Revolution could not be averted, it was a fatal thing, an explosion of moral forces as inevitable as the eruption of a volcano, which is an explosion of the physical forces of nature." [16]

Revolution is Chaos. Its destructive forces are boundless. Let loose, it would have shattered the human Cosmos to its foundations, levelled it down to that *tabula rasa,* of which sings the "Internationale." To save the Cosmos, Chaos

[12] Rémusat, III.
[13] Holland.
[14] Roederer.
[15] Chuquet, II.
[16] *Memorial,* III.

must be bridled. This is exactly what Napoleon does, and, whatever our judgment of his other deeds, we are bound to admit that this particular act is a good and even a sacred one, or as the ancients would say "godlike," for the gods were primarily the controllers and builders of Chaos.

"I closed up the chasm of anarchy; I put an end to Chaos; I cleansed the Revolution." [17]

Cosmos is nourished by Chaos. The most beautiful Cosmos is but Chaos organized: this is known to the gods; he, the pretended slayer of the Revolution but actually its god Mysogetes, knows it too.

"In spite of all its atrocities, the Revolution was the true cause of our moral regeneration; thus the most foul-smelling manure produces the most noble vegetation. Men may restrain or temporarily suppress this progress, but are powerless to crush it." [18] "Nothing can destroy or efface the great principles of the Revolution, its sublime truths will endure forever in the light of the wonderful deeds we have done, in the halo of glory with which we surrounded them! Already they are immortal! . . . They live in Great Britain, shed their light in America; have become the heritage of the French

[17] *Memorial,* II.
[18] *Memorial,* IV.

Nation. They are the torch which will illuminate the world. . . . They will become the religion of all nations and, say what you will, this new epoch will be associated with my name, because I kindled the torch and shed a light on its beginnings, and now through persecution I will be forever acclaimed as its Messiah. Friends and foes alike will call me the first soldier of the Revolution, its champion leader. When I am no more, I shall remain for all nations the beacon star of their rights, and my name will be their battle cry, the slogan of their hopes!" [19]

As Pushkin said:

> And in his gloom of exile traced
> The line of lasting liberty.

Is that so? What did he bequeath to the world, Liberty or Slavery?

The Chaos of Revolution, while sweeping away the inferior Cosmos, attains in one of its sources to the highest Cosmos; for one brief moment the half-bestial, half-godlike countenance of the Revolution is lit up by the fiery tongue of the "thrice flaming light" (*"Das dreimal glühende Licht"*) : [20] *Liberty, Equality, Fra-*

[19] *Memorial,* II
[20] Goethe, *Faust.*

ternity—the Son, Father, and Spirit. That moment gone, the light dies out, and the third member—Fraternity, that synthesis of Liberty and Equality—drops out of the trinomial formula. In place of Fraternity comes Fratricide, the rattle of the knife on the guillotine. "Fraternity or death?" (*"La fraternité ou la mort?"*) Liberty and Equality—the thesis and antithesis confront each other in an insoluble antinomy: liberty in anarchy or equality in slavery; the rule of one over all, or that of all over one; the annihilation of society by Chaos, or the suppression of the individual in an accursed Cosmos.

It may be that Napoleon had some vague conception of this antinomy; he never solved it, but merely eliminated it by sacrificing liberty to equality. "Better abolish liberty than equality. It is the spirit of the times, and I wish to be a son of my times!" [21] "Equality, nothing but equality—is the slogan which unites us to the Revolution." [22] "I wished to introduce a system of universal equality." [23] "My principal rule was to encourage all those who have talents irrespective of their birth and social position.

[21] *Memorial,* IV.
[22] Rémusat, III.
[23] O'Meara, II.

The Builder of Chaos

It is for this system of equality that I have incurred the hatred of your (British) oligarchy." [24] "Liberty is the need of the few elect. . . . It can be constrained with impunity, but equality is pleasing to the majority." [25]

In this he was mistaken. He restrained liberty, but not with impunity: her vengeance was St. Helena—lifelong captivity.

Not only the elect few but whole nations recoiled from him and rose up against him in the name of liberty. England, "the nation of shopkeepers," as he called her, revealed herself as the champion of the freedom of the world.

He was faced with a scheme of things which was to prove fatal to him. England—the Ocean-Liberty engaged in a deadly combat against Napoleon—Land-Equity. Thesis versus antithesis. But the synthesis had dropped out: the world Brotherhood of nations embracing all the continents girt by seas, a new Atlantis. "Paradise lost and regained" had failed.

When speaking in the language of men, inadequate for such as he, Napoleon seems to realize his so-called guilt before liberty. "I swear that I do not give greater freedom to

[24] O'Meara, II.
[25] Rémusat, III.

France only because I think she is better so." [26]
"My despotism? Historians will prove that dictatorship was necessary . . . anarchy, self-will,
widespread disorder still knocked at our
doors." [27] "In the midst of a host of vanquished
kings I could only be a crowned Washington.
. . . But this could not be achieved otherwise
than by a world-wide dictatorship, for which I
strove. Where then is my crime?" [28] Two days
before he died, shortly before he lost consciousness and speaking at a moment when men cease
to lie: "I sanctified all the principles of the
Revolution, I embodied them in my laws and
deeds. . . . Unfortunately, circumstances were
cruel and compelled me to be cruel pending
better times. . . . Then misfortunes set in, I
could not loosen the bow-string, and France was
deprived of those free institutions which I had
planned for her." [29]

That Napoleon under any circumstances
could become a Washington is scarcely probable. Still, he may be less guilty against liberty
than it appeared to his contemporaries.

Liberty and equality are emanations from
the same power; they are the light and warmth

[26] Roederer.
[27] *Memorial,* II.
[28] *Memorial,* I.
[29] Lacour-Gayet.

proceeding from one and the same sun. There is no true equality without freedom or without at least a spark of it; and Napoleon's "road open to ability," the foundation of modern democracy, is true equality. Mankind, as a rule, is unable to sustain too great a measure of freedom, yet it cannot live wholly without it. An exceedingly small dose of it was ingrained in the Napoleonic Code, but it took root so firmly and surely that the whole European civilization must collapse ere men will suffer themselves to be deprived of it.

Democracy is an indifferent sort of paradise, but those who have been in hell know that even an indifferent paradise is better than hell, and that the scant liberty of a democracy as compared with the absolute slavery of communism is like the freshness of a spring morning compared with the icy circle of Dante's *Inferno* or the cold of inter-planetary space.

Perhaps, nowadays, Russians who have tasted of the communist inferno know of Napoleon that which Europeans do not, and which cannot be learnt from forty thousand books.

"I had to be victorious in Moscow." [30] "I should have attained everything had it not been for the burning of Moscow.[31]

[30] *Memorial*, I.   [31] O'Meara, I.

Napoleon

1812–1917. The former year marked the beginning, the latter saw the end; perhaps the one would not have happened without the other. "I would have emancipated the serfs in Russia." [32] Had he done so, perhaps the Russian revolution, the Russian *inferno* would not have been.

Who set fire to Moscow? Russian patriots? No, robbers, murderers and bandits let loose from the prison. [33] "Men with the faces of devils amid the roaring flames—a veritable image of the *inferno*," [34] writes Ségur.

"What a people! What a people! They are Scythians!" Napoleon kept repeating horror-struck. "Scythians with squinting greedy eyes" [35] ready to hurl themselves on Rome like wolves on a carcass. Napoleon knew this, he alone of all Europeans.

> Bright sun of Austerlitz depart!
> Rise, our great Moscow, rise in flames! [36]

Moscow rose in flames, and the prophecy was fulfilled.

"What a calamity is my fall! I tied up the

[32] O'Meara.
[33] Ségur, III.
[34] Ségur.
[35] A. Block, *The Scythians.*
[36] Pushin, *Napoleon,* 1821, transl. by Sir B. Pares.

skin with the winds, but it has again been pierced by an enemy bayonet. I might have calmly set about regenerating the world, but now it will be accomplished only in the midst of storms." [37]

"Russians are barbarians without a fatherland, who prefer every country to that in which they were born.[38]

"People will remember me, when the Russian barbarians will overrun Europe, which would not have happened without your aid, *messieurs les Anglais!*" [39] We may now add: "without yours, *messieurs les Européens.*"

"You will weep tears of blood over me!" "France had greater need of me than I of her!" [40] This saying of Napoleon's still remains an enigma for France, but not for Russia.

He was not quite just in his estimate of Russians. Not all of them are "barbarians"; there are among them such as love Europe and know it better perhaps than the Europeans themselves.

Even so, Russians now see that which is invisible to Europeans: tremendously high above us—the dizzy height giving us a measure of the

[37] *Memorial*, II.
[38] O'Meara, I.
[39] O'Meara.
[40] *Memorial*, III.

depth of the abyss into which we have been hurled—across the mountains of the West rides a Horseman, his dark figure sharply outlined against the lurid, flaming sky. Who is he? One cannot mistake him.

> He wears the grey coat of a soldier,
>   And a little cocked hat on his head. . . .[41]

Slowly he rides, his gaze fixed on the far-off East, his gleaming sword in his hand—ever keeping watch. Over what is he keeping watch and against whom? Europeans know not, Russians do; he guards holy Europe from the Red Devil.

[41] Lermontov.

Chapter III

THE LORD OF THE WORLD

"THE idea of a universal Union of all men is the idea of European mankind; its civilization grew out of it, and it is the aim of its life," says Dostoievsky in his "Diary of a Writer" and he again repeats it in the "Brothers Karamazov" in the Great Inquisitor's narrative of Christ's three temptations in the desert—with bread, miracles, and power: "The desire for an universal unity is mankind's final torment. Mankind as an entity always aspired to be organized on an universal basis. There existed many great nations with great histories, but the more civilized were these peoples, the more they were unhappy, for the keener they realized the need for such an universal unity."

Dostoievsky is right; the eternal and cardinal torment of mankind is this quenchless yearning after universality.

It may appear at first sight, that the only real entities in history are national bodies—"peo-

ples, races, nations." Yet a deeper study will
reveal them to be in a state of continuous struggle against themselves and each other; they try
to overcome both themselves and one another
for the sake of creating some higher super-
national and universal entity. They are all, more
or less, conscious of being but "scattered members," (*"membra disjecta"*) of some body which
once was and will be again. They all move
through history, and writhe like the vertebræ
of a snake that is cut into pieces but not killed,
striving to be joined together again; or like
the dry bones in the field seen by Ezekiel: "And
. . . there was a noise, and behold a shaking
and the bones came together, bone to his bone
. . . but there was no breath in them."

From the days of "Sargon the Ancient"—
Sarganissar, king of Babylon, founder of the
first world monarchy (about 2800 B. C.) to the
Third International, the process of universal
history is but the writhing of these snake-
vertebræ, the noise of these dry bones.

As far back as human memory is able to
reach, mankind was tortured by that quenchless
yearning after universality. The ancient world-
monarchies—Egypt, Babylon, Assyria, Media,
Persia, Macedonia, were so many attempts at its

fulfillment, endeavours "to organize themselves on the principle of universality." One and the same idea unites the two halves of mankind— the Pagan and the Christian. Christianity could only be accomplished within the Helleno-Roman universality; not by chance was the Son of Man born within the world-wide territory of Rome, under the world sceptre of the Roman Cæsar.

The idea of universality inaugurated by pagan Rome is carried on by Christian Rome down to our own times, until the Revolution. The Revolution seceded from Christianity in everything save in the idea of universality. "As a matter of fact the French Revolution was nothing more than the last variation and re-incarnation of the same ancient Roman formula of universal unity," so writes Dostoievsky, but does not say all.

The last incarnation of universality was not the Revolution, not Chaos, but its dominator— Napoleon.

To achieve this universality was the principal, if not the sole, task of his whole life. If one fails to realize this, his life becomes unintelligible. All his deeds, thoughts, and feelings start and end here. "Thirst for world-dominion is part of his nature; it can be thwarted or side-tracked but cannot be destroyed," was Metternich's shrewd comment on Napoleon.[1] And again: "My opinion of Napoleon's secret schemes and designs never changed: his monstrous aim always was and is—the subjugation of the whole continent to the rule of one." [2]

Why is that aim "monstrous"? Why call Napoleon's world-dominion "subjugation"? Because he is the most "ambitious" and "power-loving" man the world has ever seen.

To blame Napoleon for his love of power is like blaming a sculptor for loving his marble, or a musician for loving sound. The crux of the question lies not in whether he loves power, but why he loves it and what he makes of it.

Love of power is a strong passion, but not the strongest. Of all human passions the most fiery and one that rules supreme and consumes the soul with transcendent fire, is the passion of thought. And of all passionate ideas the most passionate was that which held sway over him —"mankind's last torment," its quenchless yearning—the idea of universality. Perhaps it is no longer a passion, but something superior to it, for which we can find no suitable expression,

[1] Lacour-Gayet.
[2] Taine; Metternich, II.

for, as Mme. de Staël rightly says, "Words fail
to define Napoleon's personality."

He himself owns: "I wanted world-dominion
and who, placed as I was, would not? The world
called me to power. Kings and subjects all vied
with one another to come beneath my sceptre." [3]

He might have said of the world as he said
of France: "The world stood more in need of
me than I of it."

If that is "love of power" and "ambition,"
they are of an order different from ours which
cannot be defined by human words. He himself
is almost unaware of possessing them. "I had no
ambition . . . and even if I had, it was inborn
in my nature, and is a part of myself as the blood
flowing in my veins or the air which I
breathe!" [4] "My ambition? It was of the highest
and noblest kind that ever perhaps existed—that
of establishing and consecrating the Empire of
reason, and the full exercise and enjoyment of
all human faculties." [5]

The Empire of reason—the universal Empire. What means does he use to reach his goal?

"One of my greatest ideas was the gathering
together of peoples who form geographical en-

[3] *Memorial.*
[4] Roederer.
[5] *Memorial,* II.

tities but are divided and dismembered by politics and revolutions. . . . I wanted to create a single national body out of each!" [6] Such is the beginning, while the goal: the unification of national bodies into a universal body; "a European League of Nations" (*"Association Européenne."*) [7]

"It would have been a noble thing to have advanced into posterity with such a train, and attended by the blessings of future ages. . . . Only then could one indulge in the chimera of a beau-ideal of civilization—in a unity of codes, principles, opinions, sentiments, views, and interests." [8] "A pan-European code of laws, pan-European judicial system, currency, weights, and measures." "Navigation on the rivers free to all, an universal freedom of the seas." [9] General disarmament, the end of all wars, universal peace. "The whole population of Europe would have become as one family, and every man, while he travelled abroad, would still have found himself at home." [10]

"Then at last, by the help of the universal diffusion of knowledge, one might have thought

[6] *Memorial*, IV.
[7] *Memorial*, III.
[8] *Memorial*, IV.
[9] *Memorial*, III.
[10] *Memorial*, IV.

of attempting in the Great European family the application of the American Congress or the Amphictyone of Greece. What a perspective of power, grandeur, happiness, and prosperity would thus have appeared!"

How near it all seemed, so near that one had but to stretch out a hand to grasp it. Twice did he stretch it out. He made two attempts at universal "regeneration." "The first from the south through England—the republican; the second from the north, through Russia—the monarchical. Both aimed at one goal and it would have been accomplished with firmness, good faith, and moderation. What calamities, known and unknown, would not unhappy Europe have escaped! Never had a project so favourable to the interests of civilization been conceived, or so near being carried into execution. It is a remarkable fact that the obstacles which occasioned my failure were not the work of men but proceeded from the elements! In the south the sea frustrated my plans; the burning of Moscow, the snow and the winter completed my ruin in the north. Thus water, air, and fire—all Nature was hostile to the universal regeneration which Nature herself called for. The mysteries of Providence are unfathomable." [11]

[11] *Memorial*, I.

"Nevertheless, sooner or later the nations will become united by the very force of events: the impulse is given, and I think that since my fall and the destruction of my system no grand equilibrium can possibly be established in Europe except by the concentration and confederation of the principal nations." [12]

"You may ask like Pyrrhus' counsellor: what is the use of it all? I will tell you: to found a new social order and avert great catastrophes. All Europe is waiting for it and demands it. The old order has collapsed and the new is coming into being amid terrible and prolonged convulsions." [13]

Never had Napoleon's words sounded so prophetically as they do now. 1814–1914. The two dates answer each other across time. The one marks the fall of that beginning of universality —the Empire of Napoleon; the other—the outbreak of the World War. Mankind has just passed through "terrible convulsions"; and others, perhaps more terrible still, may yet be in store, according to his own prophecy: "a single spark may set the world aflame." And our only safeguard lies in that pitiable shadow

[12] *Memorial*, IV.
[13] *Ibid.*

of universality, the soul of a babe unborn hovering in Limbo, the still-born League of Nations.

To realize the full portent of universality to Napoleon, one must remember that to him it was no abstract idea but a thing of flesh and blood; not a "something" which was to be, but which existed within him. One must realize that Napoleon was not a man possessed by the idea of universality, but himself a cosmic being, or in the words of Dostoievsky, "a premature pan-man." In this, as in much else, he was "a being unlike any other," according to Mme. de Staël's profound remark.

He was the contemporary not of his own times, but either of an immemorial past when "the whole earth was of one language, and of one speech"—one human family; or of an immeasurably far-off future, when "there shall be one fold and one shepherd." He is, as it were, a being of a different cycle of creation, either too ancient or too new, prehistoric or apocalyptic.

He is a man without a fatherland, not through deficiency but rather from an excess of "something." In his youth he loved his native Corsica and wanted to be a "patriot" like the Corsican hero Paoli or like Plutarch's heroes. He did not succeed in this, and was soon proclaimed "an enemy of the fatherland" and banished by his fellow countrymen.

He was himself aware of this trait in himself and marvelled at it; to the very end he frankly acknowledged that he did not know who he was. "I am more of an Italian or Tuscan than a Corsican." [14] "I *wanted* at all costs to be a Frenchman. Being called a 'Corsican' was to me the bitterest of insults." [15] "A mayor, I think it was in Lyons, thought to pay me a compliment by saying: 'It is marvellous how much Your Majesty, not being a Frenchman, loves France!' It was as if he had struck me with a stick!" [16]

"Whatever language he speaks it always sounds like a foreign tongue; he appears to force it to express his thought." [17] "Bonaparte's incorrect pronunciation (in French) was a great drawback to state occasions. In general he had his speech drawn up for him . . . and he would be instructed in the proper pronunciation of the words; but when he came to speak he forgot his lesson, and in a muffled voice with lips scarcely parted would read the speech in an accent more

[14] Gourgand, II.
[15] *Ibid.*
[16] *Ibid.*
[17] Rémusat, I.

strange even than it was foreign and more un-
pleasant. The indisputable testimony of his
accent to the fact that he was a foreigner struck
painfully on the ear and the mind alike." [18]

This is what it means to be a man possessing
no mother-tongue, no nation, no fatherland.

Does he love France? Assuredly he does!
Yet even so clear-sighted a man as Stendhal is
mistaken in thinking he loves her as his fatherland. He himself commits that error. "I swear
that I do everything for the sake of France
alone." [19] "In happiness and misfortune, on the
fields of battle, in council, on the throne, and in
exile—France was the constant object of all my
thoughts and deeds." [20] "All for the sake of the
French people," was his bequest to his son. Yet
has he himself given of his all to the people?

What is a fatherland? It is one's native country separated by frontiers from other peoples'
countries. And the whole aim of the Napoleonic
wars was to expand indefinitely and finally to
abolish the frontiers of France. "When France
becomes Europe, she will cease to be France,"
he is warned. [21] That is exactly what he aims at:

[18] Rémusat, III.
[19] Roederer.
[20] Houssaye, *1815*.
[21] Ségur, IV.

there will be no France—there will be the universe.

"What splendid troops!" the Prussian Marshal V. Mellendorf exclaimed admiringly at a French army review held in conquered Berlin in 1807. "Yes, splendid," replied Napoleon,— "if only they could be made to forget their native land." [22]

"He has so far corrupted the nature of the French army that it has lost all national memory," [23] writes a woman contemporary of Napoleon. "The Little Corporal" means more to his soldiers than France; where he is, there is the fatherland. Napoleon's army, like himself, already has become a cosmic being.

He does not always err, however, concerning his patriotism. "I have one passion, one mistress —France: I lie with her (*je couche avec elle*). She has never been untrue to me; she pours out her blood for me and lavishes her gold upon me." [24] Men do not speak so of their native country: to them she is not the mistress but the mother; it is not she who sacrifices all to them, but they to her.

At best France is his mistress, at worse—a

[22] Thiébault, III.
[23] Rémusat, III.
[24] Roederer.

war charger, that marvellous nag of which the poet sings. The frenzied rider rode her to death.

> Mourante, elle tomba sur un lit de mitraille
> Et du coup te cassa les reins.[25]

And most marvellous of all—were France, in her death throes, asked whether she would prefer never to have had Napoleon as her frenzied rider, perhaps, her answer would be—"No, I would not!" And therein lies France's greatness.

Neither a Corsican, nor an Italian, nor a Frenchman, perhaps not even a European. Europe was for him but the route to Asia. "Your Europe is a mole-hill! Only in the East have there been great empires and mighty upheavals; in the East, where dwell six hundred million people." [26]

The lure of the East grips him all his life. In Egypt, before the Syrian campaign, young General Bonaparte poring for hours on the ground over huge outspread maps, dreams of a march to India across Mesopotamia following the route of Alexander the Great.[27] Had his dream come true, the last founder of a world monarchy would have confronted his prede-

[25] Barbier, *La Cavale.*
[26] Bourrienne, I.
[27] *Ibid.*

cessor across forty-five countries—the Babylonian king Sarganissar; both followed the same route: only the one came from East to West, and the other—from West to East.

"With overwhelming forces I shall enter Constantinople, overthrow the Sultan, and found a new and great empire of the Orient. This will bring me immortal fame,"[28] he rhapsodises pacing the beach at St. Jean d'Acre. "Had Acre fallen, the French army would have made its way to Aleppo and Damascus by forced marches and speedily reached the Euphrates. . . . We should have enlisted six hundred thousand Christians and who knows what would have happened then? I should have gone to India and changed the face of the world . . ."[29] he recalls his dreams again at St. Helena.

After the 18th Brumaire, no sooner had he seized power, than he offers the Emperor Paul I of Russia a joint campaign against India, and later, at the summit of his fame after Tilsit, he repeats the proposal to Alexander I.

Says he in 1811, a few months before the Russian campaign: "It is a long route, but after all it leads to India. To reach the Ganges Alex-

[28] Bourrienne, I.
[29] *Memorial*, II.

ander (the Great) had as far to go as I from Moscow. . . . From the confines of Europe I must enter Asia in order to strike at England (in India). . . . This of course is a gigantic enterprise, but achievable in the nineteenth century."[30]

The imperial baggage contained a special van with coronation apparel, crown, state sword and mantle. It was rumoured that Napoleon intended to be crowned a second time in the sacred town of Delhi on the banks of the Ganges, as the Emperor of the East and West.

On the eve of Borodino a portrait of his son and heir was brought from Paris: the child in his cradle playing with an imperial sceptre surmounted by the terrestrial globe.

In 1811, the Emperor sends the Minister of Marine, Decrès, a scheme for the construction, within three years, of two fleets: one an ocean fleet with its base in Ireland, and one for the Mediterranean to be stationed in Egypt and Sicily. Expeditions are planned to the Cape of Good Hope, to Surinam, Martinique and other lands beyond the seas. The fleets will be distributed in both hemispheres to consolidate world dominion not only over Europe and Asia

[30] Lacour-Gayet.

but over the entire universe. "Five years hence I shall be the lord of the world," he said in that same year of 1811.[31]

"The Emperor is mad, stark mad!" [32] Decrès kept repeating, horror-struck. This indeed is bordering on insanity. Never had any man, neither Sargon, nor Alexander, nor Cæsar ever conceived such a blindingly clear perception of world dominion.

It seems at times as if he himself fears his own thoughts; though "fear" is too human a word to be applied to him; in any case, he feels their fateful burden.

Everything he does tends towards his goal, though he seldom mentions it. "I always realized the necessity of mystery, he says at St. Helena when he knows that all is over and the game is up! "I always realized that my ends could best be served by surrounding myself with a halo of mystery which has such a strong fascination for the multitude. It fires the imagination, paves the way to those brilliant and dramatic effects which give one such power over men. This was the cause of my unfortunate march to Moscow. Had I been more deliberate

[31] Abbé de Pradt. *Histoire de l'Ambassade dans le Grand Duché de Varsovie en 1812.*
[32] Marmont, *Mémoires,* III.

I might have averted every evil, but I could not delay it. It was necessary that my movement and success should seem, as it were, supernatural." [33]

He had need of the "mysterious," the "supernatural"; this means, he needs religion. His thoughts having reached some extreme point in his scheme of world dominion, he suddenly realized how impossible it was for him to do away with religion, that mankind could not be universally united otherwise than round some inner centre, the Absolute Unity—God.

"I created a new religion. Already I pictured myself on the road to Asia riding on an elephant, with a turban on my head, and carrying a new Alcoran written by myself." [34] This of course is uttered in a sarcastic vein. He is too intelligent not to know that Alcorans cannot be invented, nor religions created.

It should be remembered that always he speaks of this in an offhand, detached sort of way, as it were, from the "outside"; not superficially, because his sayings are often very profound, but as if the matter was no concern of his, and with a mocking smile reminding one of the sneer on the skull of the philosopher of

[33] *Memorial,* IV.
[34] Rémusat, I.

Ferney, though he has neither sympathy nor respect for Voltaire.

"He is a bad man, an evil man! it is he who brought us to this," he might have said of him with even greater relish than of Rousseau. Withal he is unable to dispense with a Voltairesque sneer at religion. Behind it, however, one feels, there lurks the consciousness that religion to him is no mere trifle, but something tremendously vital, important and, again using a human expression so unsuitable for the like of him, so "awe-inspiring."

Whatever his attitude, but once having realized that world dominion cannot exist without religion, he realized that its religious structure must assume the shape of a pyramid, narrowing towards the summit till finally it ends in a single mathematical point where earth touches heaven, and man meets God. In other words, man, when once he reaches the pinnacle of world dominion, is *bound*—whether he wills it or not—to utter the awful, or perhaps foolish, "insane" words: "I am God."

"Divus Cæsar Imperator." The Roman Cæsars uttered them not through foolishness, nor yet out of "satanic pride," for did they not number men as brilliant as Julius Cæsar or saints like Antoninus Pius or Marcus Aurelius. They were compelled to do so by the inner logic of world dominion: once having attained to this high place, man was *bound* to say it—otherwise the entire pyramid would collapse from under him.

With his geometrical clearness of vision Napoleon realized this. "As soon as a man becomes king, he is a separate being from his fellow-men. I always admired Alexander's (the Great) sound political instinct which prompted him to proclaim his divine origin." [35] "Superior to all Alexander's victories ranks his 'great policy'—the visit to the temple of Amon, where the priest whispers in his ear: 'thou art son of God.' " [36]

Alexander and Cæsar could do this before the birth of Christ. What about doing the same after? This Napoleon does not seem to know. At times he thinks it might be tried. "Had I returned from Moscow as a conqueror, I should have had the world at my feet, all nations would have admired and blessed me. I might have withdrawn myself mysteriously from the world, and popular credulity would have revived the fable of Romulus; it would have said

[35] Rémusat, I.
[36] Gourgaud, II.

that I had been carried up to heaven to take my place among the gods!" [37]

At other times he seems to doubt the possibility of this:

"I have come into the world too late. There is nothing great left for me to do"—he tells Decrès,—the very man who feared the Emperor "had gone mad,"—on the 2nd of December, 1804, his Coronation Day: "Of course I have had a brilliant career, but what a difference between me and the heroes of antiquity! Look at Alexander, for instance. After he had conquered Asia he declares himself to be the son of Jupiter, and except Olympia his mother, and Aristotle and a few Athenian pedants, the whole East believes him. Now, were I to declare myself the son of the Father Almighty and order a thanksgiving service on the occasion, every fish-wife in Paris would jeer at me to my face. No, people are too civilized nowadays. There is nothing great left for me to do!" [38]

Now he can, and then he cannot. Here his geometrical clearness of vision plays him false. The portals of the "dark hemisphere" close round him, and "the state of continual enlight-

[37] *Memorial,* IV.
[38] Marmont, II.

enment" in which he lived according to Goethe,
seems to abandon him. He is obliged to grope
his way to avoid "ridicule": "there is but a step
from the sublime to the ridiculous." Here a
fish-wife's jeer may trip up the lord of the
world.

Dimly he sees, or merely hears, that somewhere, quite close, almost at his side, there is
being built another pyramid of world dominion. Could he see more clearly he would
have realized that this second pyramid was being raised not alongside but above his own, and
that the two opposed each other. One, his own
—that of pagan Rome, *Imperium Romanum*
was rising from earth to heaven; the second—
that of the Christian City of God descended
from heaven to earth. Their pinnacles touched
at a point, at which according to the meaning
of the lower pyramid man becomes God, and
to that of the higher—God becomes Man; the
one sacrifices universe to himself, the other
offers Himself in sacrifice for the world.
Napoleon had some vague perception of this
antinomy; for when he himself was crucified on
the rock of St. Helena, had he not voiced this no
longer with a sneer but in solemn earnest, when
he said: "Jesus Christ would not have been the

Son of God, if He had not died on the Cross."

He should have fixed his choice on one of the two pyramids. But this is precisely what he does not: he is afraid; here at least the use of this human world seems appropriate to him. He wants to unite both pyramids. The Concordat is an attempt in that direction.

"It was the supreme victory over the spirit of the Revolution; all the rest were but the outcome of this, the principal one. The success of the Concordat was a proof of how clearly Bonaparte had read what was in the heart of the people." [39]

Yes, he understood that religions could not be created nor Alcorans invented; he refused to be that "portentous mixture of Quack and Prophet" with which epithet Carlyle had dismissed him with such crude levity. "Would you like me to invent some new and unknown religion according to my fantasy? No, I hold a different view on the matter. I need the old Catholic faith; it alone retains its grip on all hearts, and alone can turn the hearts of the people towards me and remove all obstacles from my path." [40]

[39] Pasquier, *Mémoires,* I.
[40] Pasquier, *Mémoires.*

Yet he knows that religion itself is the greatest obstacle of all. "Christianity is incompatible with the state," wrote the seventeen-year-old Bonaparte in his boyish diary. "The kingdom of Christ is not of this world. It places the supreme power of God above the sovereign rule of the people,"—he might have added: "and of that of the monarch." "It destroys the unity of the state." [41]

To join together church and state, the two pyramids of world dominion, it is necessary to bring about some fundamental change in Christianity itself. What kind of change? "My first care was not to touch dogma," Napoleon says naïvely with a soldier's off-hand way of dismissing "civilian" matters.[42] But not to touch dogma was no easy matter; in fact it was more difficult than he thought: for is not the very substance of dogma contained in the question: Who is the true Lord of the World, the God-man or the man-god?

He, nevertheless, attempted to solve this strenuous problem. He proclaimed that there were not two vicars of Christ—the Pope and Emperor, but one alone—the Cæsar. According to the Napoleonic catechism,—"God made the

[41] Masson, *Manuscrits.*
[42] *Memorial,* III.

Emperor His viceregent and His image on earth."[43] Is it an image only? Did not the Archbishop of Rouen blasphemously playing with the word *"christos" "the anointed,"* call the Emperor "the Christ of Providence." *"le christ de la Providence"*? [44]

"I hoped to rule the Pope, and what immense influence I should then wield! What powerful means at my disposal for governing the world!" —Once again, at St. Helena when all is over and the game lost, does Napoleon disclose his "mystery" plans.[45] "I should have governed the religious with the same facility as the political world."[46] "I intended to exalt the Pope beyond measure, to surround him with grandeur and honours. I should have succeeded in suppressing all his anxiety for the loss of his temporal power. *I should have made an idol of him;* he would have remained near my person. Paris would have become the capital of Christendom and I should have governed the religious as well as the political world." [47] Always he harps upon the subject, returning to it again and again.

[43] Rémusat, III.
[44] Lacour-Gayet.
[45] *Memorial,* III.
[46] *Ibid.*
[47] *Ibid.*

The Lord of the World

Is this task easy to carry out? He is not sure. "The control of religion in the hands of sovereigns had been for a long time the constant object of my meditations and wishes. . . . No government can be carried on without it. . . . But the task was extremely difficult; at every step I was alive to the danger. I was induced to think that once engaged in it, I should be abandoned by the nation." [48] The "fish-wife's jeer" once more!

And worst of all, he is at a loss what to do with the Pope. He fights a phantom with a sword. He alternately cajoles and wounds him. "Pius VII is a regular lamb, an absolutely good man, I have great esteem and sympathy for him." [49]

Thus the beginning of their intercourse, and here is the end: "the pope is a frenzied imbecile, who ought to be locked up." [50] And lock him up he does: first in Savona and later in Fontainebleau.

The Pope refused to become an "idol." The lamb turned out to be a lion, and the soft wax— a firm rock, the very same of which it has been said: "upon this rock I will build My church."

[48] *Memorial,* III.
[49] *Ibid.*
[50] *Correspondence,* XIX, 15.

73

Napoleon

"We have done all to preserve good understanding,"—Pius VII wrote of the Concordat, —"and were willing to do still more, provided those principles were left untouched, upon which we are immutable. For where our conscience is at stake, nothing can move us, were even our skin torn off our body." [51]

The outcome of this war, the greatest perhaps ever waged by Napoleon, defies imagination, had not the end come with appalling swiftness; the pyramid of world dominion crumbled into dust and he found himself hurled naked upon the bare rock of St. Helena.

Did he then at last discern Him, against Whom He wrestled as did Jacob in his sleep? "I will not let thee go, except thou bless me." God blessed Napoleon by the mouth of the holy father Pius VII: "we must not forget that after God religion owes its restoration primarily to him (Napoleon). . . . The Concordat is a Christian and heroic act of salvation." [52] No saying could be more profound and to the point: "Christian and heroic," both human and divine. That is the point of contact of the two pyramids.

He failed to join them and fell crushed be-

[51] Léon Bloy.
[52] Lacour-Gayet.

74

neath their weight. But herein lies his greatness, that in the course of two millenniums, he alone of all men endeavoured to bear that burden.

Had he a precognition of who was his tempter? If he did, it was subconsciously, in his prophetic dreams.

"And the devil taking him up into a high mountain, shewed unto him all the kingdoms of the world in a moment of time. And the devil said unto him. All this power will I give thee and the glory of them: for that is delivered unto me; and to whomsoever I will I will give it. If thou therefore wilt worship me, all shall be thine." Napoleon refused to worship Satan, and the kingdoms of the world were taken from him.

What caused his fall? He thought—Destiny. But it was not Destiny which betrayed him, but he himself. He, the mighty one, suddenly recognized his weakness before the power of a Mightier One, and therein, perhaps, lies his supreme claim to greatness.

So he dies, all unknowing of Him Who had vanquished him. Unlike the great Apostate of old he was not even to proclaim on his death bed: "Thou hast conquered, Galilean!" He merely bowed his head in silence; and from off that bowed head an Invisible Hand lifted the Imperial crown and laid upon it a crown of thorns.

CHAPTER IV

THE MAN FROM ATLANTIS

BEFORE Napoleon's birth, his mother Maria
Letizia Buonaparte had dedicated the child to
the Holy Virgin Mother, as if she knew with
a mother's intuition that he would stand in need
of her holy protection. And the boy was born
on the 15th of August, on the day of the As-
sumption of Our Lady.

Did Napoleon ever give a thought to the significance of this dedication? That is unlikely.
Even if he did, it probably appeared to him,
as to us, incongruous—he, of all men, to be
dedicated to the Holy Virgin!

As it turned out, this dedication was not as ill-
fitting as it seemed, though not in the sense ap-
proved of by "good Catholics," or even by
Christians in general, but as interpreted by the
ancient pre-Christian worshippers of the Great
Mother of the Gods, Magna Mater Deorum.
Long before the Christian era she reigned supreme here in Corsica and in all the islands and

seaboard of the Mediterranean. Here, in the earliest cradle of the human race, mankind already in its prehistoric infancy listened to Her crooning songs, lulled by the music of the waves. Mother Isis of Egypt, Ishtar-Mami of Babylon, Ashtoreth of Canaan, Virgo Cœlestis of Carthage, Rea-Cybela of Asia Minor, the Grecian Demeter—Mother Earth, and Urania—the Celestial Mother—under names and images innumerable, it is always She, the Undefiled Virgin Mother.

"Antiquam exquerite Matrem: Seek ye the Ancient Mother"; this bequest of Æneas the forefather Napoleon fulfilled as none before him. Her he sought as his beloved, her he wished to embrace—not little Corsica alone, nor little France nor yet little Europe, but the whole great Mother Earth.

And yet he knew not, or forgot, that Mother Earth is one and the same as the Mother in Heaven. Yet all his life long he harkened to her mystic call in the chime of church bells.

"I always loved the sound of village bells," [1] he said at St. Helena. "I never could fathom the impression produced on Bonaparte by the sound of church bells," wrote his schoolfellow

[1] *Memorial*, III.

The Man from Atlantis

Bourrienne. "It fascinated him. How often at Malmaison, as we paced the walk leading to the Ruelle valley, our discussions on grave affairs of state would cease at the sound of the church bell. He would pause, lest its silvery chime be deadened by the noise of our footsteps and was almost angry with me for not sharing his feelings! The fascination produced on him by these sounds was so intense, that his voice would quiver with emotion as he said to me: "this reminds me of my youth at school in Brienne, how happy I was then!" [2]

Of all earthly sound he prefers these two, the very antithesis of each other; the roar of the cannon and the chime of the village bells.

Christian legends tell of lonely wayfarers lost in the wilderness and guided to the right path by the mystical ringing of invisible bells. Napoleon did not follow the call of the bell, never even heard it; he never possessed that knowledge of himself which his mother had of him long before he was born. "Napoleon, who lived wholly for ideas, was nevertheless unable to grasp the nature of ideal motives; he repudiated the ideal, denied that there was any such thing, at the very time when he himself

[2] Bourrienne, I.

was eagerly trying to realize the ideal," says Goethe.[3]

How strange! One of the most brilliant intellects, and if one is to judge of intellect by his capacity to get to the very root of actual phenomena, the most intelligent man for at least the last two millenniums, Napoleon is yet unable to visualize, conceive and grasp his own ideal, so vast that "he lived wholly" for it. How can this be?

> Zwei Seelen wohnen, ach! in meiner Brust!
> (There dwell, alas, twin souls within my breast!)

The day-soul and the night-soul. The thoughts of the night-soul like stars in sunshine, pale in the light of day. The sun must set before the stars shine forth. But Napoleon's sun never sets: "He was in a state of continual enlightenment," it was Goethe too who said this. That is why he cannot see the stars—his night thoughts. Who knows, perhaps they are awakened by the tolling of the bell.

On the 13th of October, 1809, soon after Wagram, Napoleon held a review in Schön-

---

[3] "Napoleon, der ganz in der Idee liebte, konnte sie doch im Bewusstsein nicht erfassen; er leugnet alles seelle durchans und spricht ihm jede Wirklichkeit ab, indessen er eifrig es zu verwiklichen trachtet."

brunn near Vienna. A young man of eighteen, almost a boy, "with a pale, delicate, girlish face, Friedrich Staps by name, the son of a Protestant pastor from Naumburg, penetrates into the courtyard, is seized by the guard and searched. A large kitchen knife clumsily wrapped up in paper protrudes from his pocket. With this knife he intended to stab Napoleon, to whom he confessed at once when brought into his presence.

"Why did you want to kill me?"

"Because you have ruined my country."

"You must be mad or ill. Call Corvisart!"

Corvisart, the Emperor's court physician, examined the youth and declared him to be perfectly sane.

"If you ask my forgiveness I will grant you your life," said Napoleon.

"I do not want your forgiveness, and my only regret is that I failed to kill you," replied Staps.

"The devil! A crime is nothing to you apparently."

"To kill you would not be a crime but a duty."

"Well, and if I pardon you nevertheless, will you be grateful to me?"

"No, I will kill you all the same."

"Napoleon was astounded," writes an eye-witness.

"These are the fruits of the teaching of the Illuminates who have infested the whole of Germany! There's nothing to be done with them; sects cannot be destroyed by guns," the Emperor remarked as Staps was being led away. "Find out and report to me on his behavior at death."

Staps died like a hero. As he stood confronting the firing party, he cried out loud: "Liberty for ever! Long live Germany! Death to the tyrant!" and fell dead.

It was long before Napoleon could forget him. "I cannot get this unfortunate youth out of my head. . . . I am at a loss what to think of him. . . . This is beyond me! (*Cela me passe!*)" [4]

What was there in that "pale and delicate" eighteen-year-old boy "with a face like a girl," the face of a hero of antiquity or of a Christian martyr, that was "beyond" Napoleon and which even his all-powerful mind failed to grasp. Why was he "astounded"? Was he suddenly put in mind of a young Jacobin of '93, named Bonaparte, who had himself professed

[4] Rapp, *Mémoires*. Bourrienne, IV. Constant, *Mémoires*, III.

what Staps might have replied to his question:
"Does crime mean nothing to you?" "What a
strange question! Without liberty, there is
neither duty nor crime. . . . The Rights of Man
are graven in indelible characters on the human
heart by the Creator." [5]

"I should have thrust a dagger into my own
father if he had tried to become a tyrant." [6]

Yes, that might have startled him, but not
that alone. He was "astounded" at suddenly
finding himself powerless against some unknown force. It was as if a flash of lightning
had revealed to him his own night-soul, the
night hemisphere of the heavens, where in days
to come, at St. Helena, there would rise above
him the Constellation of the Cross invisible in
the light of day.

Were the great heathen, Goethe, told that
those "vast ideas for which Napoleon lived
though he was unable to grasp their ideal
motives" were, if not wholly, at least half
"Christian" ideas, he would have been amazed
and refused to accept it. Still more surprised
and incredulous would have been Napoleon
himself. What, in spite of all the Pope's blessings, did he actually care about Christianity?

[5] Masson, *Manuscrits.*
[6] Fournier, *Napoléon,* I.

"Monastic humility is fatal to all virtue, strength and authority. Let the legislator proclaim that man's object in life is to attain happiness here on earth." "Theology is a sewer for every kind of error and superstition." "Instead of Catechism give the people a short course of geometry." [7] Thus, artillery-lieutenant Bonaparte, a Jacobin of '93.

And these are the views expounded or held some five years later by the commander-in-chief of the Egyptian expeditionary army: "Paris is worth a mass!" meaning thereby that the conquest of the East is worth Christianity. In Egypt Bonaparte was willing to embrace Islam. "The army would have entertained but few scruples on the subject. But what would have been the consequences! I should have turned my back on Europe, and the old civilization of the continent would have been bound up. And who would then have challenged the course of Fate in France, or the regeneration of the age!" [8] "Had I remained in the East I should probably have founded an empire like Alexander by going on a pilgrimage to Mecca." [9] "I see myself entering Asia with a

[7] Masson, *Manuscrits.*
[8] *Memorial,* II.
[9] Gourgaud, II.

turban on my head and holding a new Alcoran
invented by myself."

"It has been written in Heaven since the beginning of the world that I shall come from the
West to fulfill my destiny—to destroy the
enemies of Islam and pull down the crosses,"
he wrote in a proclamation to the Moslem
sheikhs. "Thus did I make fun of them!" In
similar fashion in Italy he made fun of the
Catholics. "I am almost a crusader, I fought
the infidel Turk." [10] "This was quackery, but of
the highest order," as if purposely teasing
Carlyle by "that portentous mixture of Quack
and Prophet." [11]

"Why should you fight me?" he asks Mus-
tapha-Pasha, made prisoner at Aboukir: "you
should fight against the infidel Russians, who
worship three gods. Whereas, I, like your own
Prophet, believe in the One God." "Would this
were in your heart, it were well," is Mustapha's
shrewd and sarcastic response.[12] Napoleon's
whole dilemma is that he himself does not know
what *is* in his heart.

When later he embraces Christianity, or
rather Roman Catholicism, this is purely an

[10] Antommarchi, I.
[11] Lacour-Gayet.
[12] Ségur, I.

outward form as a means towards attaining power.

"You and I, of course, are not religious, but the people need it." [13] "How can social order be established without religion? Society cannot exist without inequality of property, but this latter cannot exist without religion. One who is dying of hunger when his neighbour is feasting can only be sustained by the belief in a higher power which ordains that on this earth there should be rich and poor and that in another world there will be different distribution of goods." [14]

Is this atheism? No. Already he sees with the clear vision of a genius what we in spite of so much terrible experience still fail to grasp, that "the greatest foe to be feared nowadays is not fanaticism but atheism."[15]

"I re-established religion. The benefits of this act will be innumerable, because without religion people would kill each other for the possession of the sweetest pear or the most beautiful girl.[16]

---

[13] Fournier, I.
[14] Roederer.
[15] Bertaut, *Virilités.* "Ce n'est pas le fanatisme qui est l'ennemi a craindre maintenant, mais l'athéisme."
[16] Antommarchi, II.

The Man from Atlantis

Once having accepted Christianity outwardly, he does not fight against it, at least not in his inner "day" consciousness, but, as it were, passes it by.

In his youth when studying the Encyclopœdia he wrote a parallel between Jesus Christ and Apollonius of Tyana, giving preference to the latter. When later, the first Consul was reminded of this by his brother Lucien, he exclaimed laughing: "Hush! we must forget all about it! Otherwise there will be a quarrel with Rome, or I shall have to make public penance that my Concordat may not be denounced as the work of Beelzebub!" [17]

"Fancy, the Pope actually believes in Christ!" he says this in frank astonishment. "The question is, did Jesus actually ever live? None of the historians mention Him, not even Joseph Flavius." "I have come to the conclusion that Jesus never existed." He is chiefly concerned, it seems, not so much with whether Christ ever did live, but *whether His coming was necessary*.

Then suddenly would come the lightning flash. "I may claim to have a knowledge of men

[17] Chuquet, II.

. . . and so I tell you: Jesus was not a mere man!" [18] "Would this were in your heart, it were well. . . ."

In his heart there is everlasting questioning and, maybe, endless suffering: "Who am I? Whence do I come? Whither I go? . . . I had lost my faith at thirteen. Perhaps I shall get it back again, God grant! I would not oppose it, I wish it were so, because I know that therein lies supreme happiness. . . ." [19] "My intellect prevents me from believing, but the recollections of my childhood and youth bring me back to the unknown." [20] Are not these recollections the call of the mystic bell sounding deep down in his heart?

"All right! I believe all the Church tells me. . . . But there are so many religions, one is at a loss to know which is the true one. . . . Had there been but one since the world begun, I should hold it to be the true one." [21] From the beginning of the world—from the ancient Mother Earth.

Antiquam exquirite Matrem.
(Seek ye the Ancient Mother.)

[18] Gourgaud, I and II.
[19] *Memorial,* III.
[20] Bourrienne, II.
[21] O'Meara, I.

The Man from Atlantis

He sought but never found her. What prevented him? Certainly not the "abuses of the priests" nor the "Catechism in place of a short course of geometry the people stood in need of."

One day when planting beans at St. Helena he was struck by the delicate beauty of their tendrils and spoke of the Creator:[22] "After all the idea of a God is the simplest. Who created all that?"[23]

On board the *Orient* on the way to Egypt his fellow travellers, the learned members of the Institute, were discoursing on the laws of creation and denying the idea of God. Raising his hand to the starlit heavens Napoleon exclaims: "Say what you like, but who made all those?"[24]

Here is something profounder still: "There are no miracles—everything is a miracle."[25] "What is the future? the past? Ourselves, what are we? We are surrounded on all sides by a mist, which hides from us that which it is most important for us to know. Our birth, life and death—all are miraculous."[26] One day at St. Helena, as ill and suffering he sat in his bath reading the New Testament, he suddenly ex-

[22] Antommarchi, I.
[23] Gourgaud, I.
[24] Bourrienne, I.
[25] *Memorial,* II.
[26] J. Bartaut.

claimed: "I am not an atheist at all! . . . Human nature has need of the supernatural. . . . No one can be certain of what one will do *in extremis*." [27]

In his last moments he summoned a Catholic priest because he "did not want to die like a dog." And when doctor Antommarchi smiled at his words to the confessor that he "wished to die like a good Catholic," he turned him out of the room. [28]

"I die in the Apostolical Roman religion in the bosom of which I was born," so runs the opening sentence of Napoleon's testament. Does he really mean this? He does not know himself. Yet surely, though coming so near, to not Catholicism nor even Christianity but Christ Himself,—against whom is he wrestling if not against Christ? Over whom must he prevail, if not over Him, so as to become "the greatest among men," the lord of the world? His night-soul, that vast ideal "for which he wholly lives," revolves incessantly around Christ.

In his poor little room at Auxonne, the seventeen-year-old lieutenant of artillery Bonaparte writes in his diary: "Always alone in the midst of men, I go back home that I may give myself

[27] O'Meara, II.
[28] Masson, *St. Helena*.

up to my lonely dreams and to the waves of my melancholy. Whither will my thoughts tend to-night? Towards death. Yet I stand on the threshold of life and may expect to live many, many years . . . in happiness. What demon then prompts me to self-destruction. And yet what is there left for me to do in this world? . . . How far removed human beings are from nature! How base they are and contemptible! . . . Life has become a burden to me, because the men I live with and probably am doomed to live with in the future are as different from me as moonlight differs from sunshine." [29]

What are the achievements of this insignificant little lieutenant that he should thus despise his fellow-men? And what does he mean by describing all men as "moonlight," and himself alone as "sunshine"? This we do not know, but Nietzsche does. "Napoleon was the last incarnation of Apollo, the sun-god." Goethe too knows. "The life of Napoleon is the life of a demi-god; he was in a state of continual enlightenment" suffused in sunlight. But perhaps best of all this is known to the old grenadier who trudges alongside the Emperor on

[29] Masson, *Manuscrits.*

the march to the Beresina in fifty degrees of
frost. "Are you cold, *mon ami*?" "No, Sire,
when I look at you I am warm!" He knows, he
feels in every fibre of his freezing body, that
all men are cold, "lunar" beings, but the Emperor alone emanates warmth as belonging to
the sun.

The 7th September, the date of Borodino—
that battle which decided the fate of the campaign and incidentally that of Napoleon's whole
empire, coincided with the beginning of the
autumn equinox, the winter solstice. On that
day Napoleon was indisposed. "The beginning
of the equinoxial period had a bad effect on
him," explains Ségur.[30] Always he was conscious of the mystical bond between his body
and the sun. "Thy flesh is the light of the sun;
thy limbs its beauteous rays. Verily, thou proceedeth from the Sun, as a child from its
mother's womb!" Such was the incantation
chanted at the matins of Akhnaton, king of
Egypt, Son of the Sun. Three and a half millenniums later, at a night vigil of flame men
worshipped another "son of the Sun," "the Sun
of Austerlitz," the Emperor himself.

A few years after writing in his diary the

[30] Ségur, IV.

entry about "lunar" and "solar" men, when still at Auxonne, he writes a strange story, like the wanderings of a mind in delirium; it may have been a delirium after all, because at the time he was suffering from an intermittent fever peculiar to the Auxonne marshes.

The plot of the story was that of Corsican *vendetta* against the whole French nation. He then hated the French as the oppressors of his native Corsica and loved his future worst enemies— the English—because they helped the Corsicans in their war of liberation.

The hero, an Englishman,—who tells the story—sails from Livorno to Spain and is shipwrecked on a small desert island not far from Corsica, a mere barren rock incessantly lashed by furious seas. Many ships have been wrecked on this island and hence perhaps its ominous name: the Gorgon. But the Englishman, who is a misanthrope, is fascinated by the wild beauty of the spot. "Never has man lived in such a wilderness. . . . Here I may at least live in wisdom and quietude if not in happiness." With thoughts as these he falls asleep at night in a tent. He is roused by the glare of flames and someone's loud cry: "Death to thee, unfortunate man!" The tent is in flames. He barely escapes and learns that a young girl, the daughter of an old man, the sole inhabitant on Gorgon island, wanted to burn him alive. On learning that he is an Englishman, the old man welcomes him and tells him his life story.

He is a Corsican. For many years he fought against Corsica's oppressors—the Genoese, Austrians and French. When these latter finally seized the island and killed his father, mother, wife and all his children except one daughter who had disappeared, he left Corsica and settled on Gorgon island, where after many adventures he found his lost daughter. They lived here like savages among the ruins of an ancient monastery, feeding on acorns and fish.

" 'My sorrows have made me hate the light of the sun. It never shines for me. Only at night time do I breathe fresh air, because the sight of my native mountains, the erstwhile dwelling place of my free forefathers, is unbearable to me. . . . I swore upon mine altar (probably the altar of the monastery chapel among the ruins of which they live), I swore never to spare the life of a single Frenchman. When their ships are wrecked on the rocks of Gorgon we save the victims as human beings and kill them as Frenchmen.

The Man from Atlantis

" 'Last year a French postal ship was almost wrecked here. The terrible cries of the crew in distress awoke my pity. I lit a huge bonfire close to the spot where they could land and so saved them. . . . Well, and how, think you, did they show their gratitude to me? When they heard I was a Corsican, they seized me and bound me in chains. . . . Thus was I punished for my weakness. My forefathers in their wrath revenged themselves for their unavenged shadows. God, however, seeing my repentance, succoured me. The ship was delayed for seven days. Their water supply ran out. They promised me freedom if I led them to the well. I consented and they knocked off my chains. I took advantage of this and thrust a dagger in the heart of one of my companions. *For the first time that day I saw the sun—and how radiant it was!* My daughter was a captive on board the ship. I put on the uniform of the soldier I had killed and armed with his sword, two pistols and my own four daggers went on board. The captain and cabin-boy were my first victims. Later I killed all the rest. We dragged all their corpses to the foot of the altar and there we burned them. And methought the odour of this new incense was pleasing unto the Lord!' " [31]

Was it a new incense? No, a most ancient one. Only the primeval cliffs of Gorgon island could recall the days when human sacrifice was offered to Moloch, Baal, Shamash and other sun-gods, still more ancient, in times of immemorial pre-historic, perhaps ante-diluvian antiquity. Thus the Christian altar on which the offering of the bloodless Sacrifice was made in years gone by was desecrated by this sacrifice of blood. Man loses sight of the sun and lives in darkness, until like the priest of Moloch, he stabs the heart of the sacrificial human victim: then only does the sun blaze forth for him once more in all its glory.

"If I had to choose a religion, the sun as the universal lifegiver would be my god; he is the true god of the earth," says Napoleon at St. Helena; lets the words drop casually as it were, though actually he is deadly in earnest. [32]

The "lunar" goddess of Reason, to whom human sacrifice too was offered by Marat and

[31] Masson, *Manuscrits.* Only a draft copy of the story has been preserved, written rather disconnectedly and in bad French. I had to simplify the rendering and explain its contents: otherwise the terrific power of thought and feeling would be unintelligible.
[32] Gourgaud, I.

Robespierre, how pale and bloodless she was in contrast with this radiant sun-god of Napoleon! "Such a man as does not care a snap for the lives of a million men." A million human lives sacrificed already, and how many more would be immolated were he to become lord of the world!

It stands to reason that a man in whose soul thoughts like these flash like flaming meteors through the night, can be neither a Corsican, nor a Frenchman, nor an Italian, not even an European nor a man of our universally-historic period, perhaps not even of our cosmic "epoch" —æon. A denizen of other "solar" epochs, he feels suffocated in this "lunar" world, where the ageing sun itself likens the moon in pallour. Unwieldy and colossal, he inadvertently crushes human beings like some ante-diluvian monster.

"He always treated civilization a little as his enemy," Talleyrand said of Napoleon.[33] Outwardly "a little," but inwardly perhaps very much so.

Every civilization, and particularly the European, means "conventionality," "decorum," "good behaviour." "What a pity such a great man should have such bad manners!" was once

[33] Rémusat, I.

Talleyrand's comment—behind the Emperor's
back—over a foul expletive of his.[34] "He was
deficient in education and in manners. He
knows neither how to enter or leave a room; he
did not know how to make a bow, how to rise
or how to sit down. His questions are abrupt,
and so is his manner of speech . . ." writes
Talleyrand's *confidante,* Mme. de Rémusat.
"As any rigid rule becomes an insupportable
annoyance to him, and every liberty which he
takes pleases him as though it were a victory, he
would never yield even to grammar." [35] Nor to
clothes: he was unable to dress himself: his
valet dressed him as if he were a child; when
undressing at night he would throw off his
clothes and toss them on the floor as an un-
familiar and useless burden: the natural con-
dition of his body was that of antique nudity,
chaste and unashamed.[36]

Civilization is "good taste." "Good taste, is
it? That is another of those classical *bons mots*
I cannot bear!" [37] "Good taste is your personal
enemy. Could you get rid of it by cannon shot,
it would long since have ceased to exist,"

[34] Lacour-Gayet.
[35] Rémusat, I.
[36] Antommarchi, I.
[37] Lacour-Gayet.

The Man from Atlantis

Talleyrand said to him.[38] Talleyrand thinks Napoleon does not know how to be "civilized"; but perhaps he does not want to? "You, Sir, are like rubbish in a silk bag," he once told Talleyrand. Who knows but that the entire European "civilization" may have been to Napoleon nothing more than "rubbish." "When I come across all this monstrosity I sometimes want to pluck it by the tail and throw it to the dogs!" he might have said like Raskolnikov.[39]

"Free to soar through space—that is what is wanted for wings like his. If he stays here he will die," is the comment of a female contemporary shortly before his departure for Egypt. He himself realizes that he must flee: "Paris presses on me like a leaden pall."[40] Not Paris only, but the entire European civilization.

Hence the lure of the East. "In Egypt I felt myself freed from the trammels of civilization. . . . Those were the best days of my life, because the most idealistic. But fate ordained otherwise. . . . I had to return to existing social conditions"—to European civilization— "the silk bag filled with rubbish."

[38] Rémusat, I.
[39] Dostoievsky, *Crime and Punishment.*
[40] Abrantès, I.

99

Hence his love of war. "War is a *natural state, (état naturel)*," an enfranchisement, a divestment from the "leaden pall" of civilization.[41]

Hence too his love for the revolution,—which he hates and destroys, but nevertheless loves. "I have sympathy for Marat because he is sincere. He always says what he thinks. He is a character. Alone he wrestles against everybody else." [42]

Napoleon, the subduer and builder of chaos, is conscious of a raging chaos within himself, greater than the revolution. And perhaps his sublimest deed lay not in taming the external chaos, but in that he overcame this inner tumult —the "Gorgon horror." Not that he could have escaped from it by his own strength. Mother Earth saved him, or perhaps the Mother of Heaven.

What is the meaning of his "hatred of civilization?" Whither does he tend to escape? Towards "a state of nature"—or so he thought in his youthful enthusiasm for Rousseau. He was, however, too intelligent and level-headed for such fancies; the Jean-Jacques fad was soon over. "I became particularly disgusted with

[41] J. Bertaut.
[42] Gourgaud, I.

Rousseau since I knew the East. Primitive man
is a beast." [43]

If not to the "wilds," then whither would he
go? Into a different civilization, or rather into
a different historic—or perhaps cosmic universe
—æon; out of our "lunar" into a "solar" world.
What is this "solar æon"?

"There dwell, alas, twin souls within my
breast!" We as yet appear to be unconscious of
the tragic significance to ourselves of the exis-
tence of these twin souls.

Twin souls imply a dual consciousness. That
of "day"—superficial, watchful and alert; and
that of "night"—slumbering and profound. The
former moves in accordance with the law of
identities, by syllogisms and induction, and
brought to its logical conclusion lends to civilization the lifeless, "mechanical" cast we know
so well. The night consciousness follows the
laws of some mysterious logic and has its being
in premonitions, clairvoyance and intuition,
clothing civilization in a living, organic, or as
the ancients would put it, "magic" form.

"Magic," "theurgy"—the actual meaning of
these terms has been lost to us long since. As an
imperfect attempt at its explanation we might

[43] Roederer.

trace a coarse and feeble analogy with "animal instinct." Ants, building their ant-heap on a river bank, know the exact spot which will be out of reach of the floods; swallows know the route to follow to return to last year's nest two thousand miles away. And such knowledge, no less precise than the one we acquire by induction, we treat as "miraculous," and "magical." We might again point out a less coarse though still more feeble similitude in the intuition and visions of great geniuses of art and science, who attained to the consummation of their ideas not by a gradual process of induction and syllogism, but by sudden, "miraculous" flights; for it is the very "miraculousness" of genius which constitutes its peculiarity and renders it incommensurable with our everyday "mechanics." Yet all these are but feeble reminders of some stupendous reality, now obscured from us; small fractions of some vast and unknown entity.

The further we recede from our own and plunge into the depths of the great civilizations of antiquity, the clearer stands out the fact of the ebb of the mechanical-day consciousness and the proportionate growth of its organic-night counterpart, of that dark—to us—sphere of it, known by the ancients as "magic" and "theurgy." Reaching to the extreme end of these successive civilizations we come to our antipodes, our antipodal-congener double, differing in methods though congenial in aims —which are those of titanic dominion over nature—and which is embodied in that organically perfect "magic" civilization known in Plato's myth as "Atlantis."

"There was once an Island facing the Pillars of Hercules. This land was in size larger than Lybia and Asia Minor put together. The name of this island was Atlantis. . . . Then great earthquakes and floods came upon it, and in a single day and night the island of Atlantis disappeared beneath the waves," thus was the ancient tradition of Egypt told to Solon the Athenian by an old priest in Saïs, and recorded in Plato's "Timeus."

Discoursing with the members of the Institute, his learned fellow travellers on board the frigate *Muiron* on the return from Egypt in 1799, Bonaparte touched upon the probable destruction of the world by a new flood or general conflagration, and may have learned from them of the myth of Atlantis,[44] or when in Egypt they might have recalled to him the mighty

[44] Ségur, I.

"Atlantes" who had spread their dominion to the confines of Egypt." (Plato, "Critius.")

What were Napoleon's thoughts as he listened to these legends? Did an answering breath stir within his own soul?

The first world kingdom was founded by the Altantes; he aspired to found the last.

The Atlantes were sons of the Ocean, so is he.

> Ocean, thine image was stamped upon him;
> He was created by thy spirit;
> He is fathomless, potent like thee,
> Like thee by naught to be tamed.[45]

The Atlantes were islanders, so is he. Born on the island of Corsica, he died on the island of St. Helena; his first fall brought him to the island of Elba; and his whole life was spent in waging war against an island—Britain, that modern little "Atlantis"—for the sake of the future great one embracing the whole Earth girt by its ocean belt.

Yet, perhaps, the inner affinity goes deeper than mere outward similarity.

Mother Earth, Sun the Father, Man the Son —such is the religion of the Atlantes, judging by the fragmentary evidence of it preserved by

[45] Pushkin, *To the Sea,* 1824. Translated by Miss Margot R. Adamson.

the Babylonian and Sumerian-Acadian forefathers of our history—

> The cuneiform writings
> Of pre-historic sages.

"Had I to choose a religion, the sun would
be my god. . . . He is the true god of the
earth." . . . Mother Earth, Sun the Father,
Man the Son—what if this were the "one religion since the beginning of the world" for
which he craved?

The Atlantes were "organic," so is he. In
legislature he substitutes living historical experience to the abstract schematism of the
"ideologues." In strategy all mechanical theo-
ries are superseded by two organic knowledges
—penetration into the living soul of the soldier
and into the living nature of the land on which
the battle is to be fought.

Thus it is in great things, and so it is in small.
He distrusts doctors, the mechanicians of the
body as much as he mistrusts "ideologues," the
mechanicians of the brain. He does not think
in syllogisms, neither does he doctor himself
with medicines: his thoughts are clairvoyance, "intuitions," his medicine "magic," auto-
suggestion.

He accepts as a necessity the degree of

"mechanism" attained by contemporary European civilization, but declines to go further. When he was making his preparations for a landing in England in 1803, Fulton offered him the use of his newly-invented steamship. Napoleon refused. This was certainly a mistake: a fleet moving by steam would have brought him victory over the British sailing fleet and provided the key to world dominion.[46] That refusal alone is proof of his abhorrence of mechanics.

Judging by the cyclopean architecture of the Atlantes, as described by Plato, their knowledge of mechanics was in no wise inferior, if not superior, to our own. Judging by our religion—Christianity, our intuition is not less but perhaps more profound than that of the Atlantes.

In what then do we differ? In will and consciousness.

We never cease to subordinate our intuition to mechanics, nor continually to conceal our nocturnal consciousness behind the diurnal. The Atlantes do the reverse: their diurnal consciousness is being continually covered by the nocturnal as by a pall, and mechanics subordinated to intuition.

In that sense, too, Napoleon is our antipode

[46] Pasquier, I.

and an Atlante: to us mechanics are wings, but to him they are a burden which he carries when soaring upon the wings of intuition.

The soul of Atlantis is "magic," but so is Napoleon's. "Great was my material power, but my spiritual domination was infinitely greater—it bordered on magic." "It was essential to me that my successes, my destinies, had something in them of the *supernatural*." And after Waterloo he said: "The *miraculous* in my destiny is in the descendant." [47]

"He possessed a "kind of *magnetic foresight* (*prévision magnétique*), of his coming destiny," says Bourrienne.[48] "I had an inner premonition of what would befall me," [49] he would say himself. It may be said that the essence of Napoleon's entire genius lay in that "inner consciousness," that "magnetic," "magical premonition"; for it was that which gave him his boundless, compelling, truly "magic" sway over both events and his fellow-men.

"*Sire, vous faîtes toujours des miracles!*" "Sire, you always work miracles!" is the naïve but profound tribute paid to him by the deputy mayor of Macon an eye-witness of that miracle,

[47] *Memorial,* IV.
[48] Bourrienne, IV.
[49] *Memorial,* IV.

the triumphal march of the Emperor from Elba
to Paris in 1815.[50]

"Thank goodness, he's fairly blown up!" was
somebody's joyous comment in 1801 after the
explosion of the infernal machine in the rue
Nikèze. "He blown up?" exclaimed an old
soldier, an Austrian, who had witnessed the
"miracles" of the Italian campaign. "Ah, you
know a great deal about it! I venture to say that
he is, at this very moment, as well as any of us.
I know him and his tricks of old!"[51] which
means: "wizard tricks," "magic."

The power of "magic" is the power of "suggestion." "When he wanted to seduce, his manner was one of ineffable charm, a kind of magnetic power,"[52] writes Ségur.

The Russian poet Tyutchev calls him a "prophetic magician," and the Egyptian Mamelukes
surnamed him "the wizard."[53]

"I fail to understand why that devil of a man
has such power over me" . . . General Vandamme confessed to a friend: "I fear neither
God nor devil, and yet when I approach him,
I am trembling all over; he could force me to

[50] Houssaye, *1815,* I.
[51] *Memorial,* IV.
[52] Ségur, IV.
[53] Lacroix.

pass through a needle's eye and throw myself
into flames!"

"Wherever I went I could only command.
. . . I was born to it. . . ." [54] said Napoleon of
himself, and men knew it.

> "And it seemed like a god from on high
>   He soared, watching o'er all, above them:
> With the light of his wondrous eyes,
>   The moving spirit of all." [55]

The gaze of a "magician" "which pierces
though one's brain,—*ses regards qui traversent
la tête*" [56] what a terrible power of suggestion—
of "magic," there is in that gaze!

Yes, indeed, a "wizard" a "great magician,"
wielding his own and other men's lives, and
shaping the history of the world into one continuous miracle.

And the meaning of all this is: the soul of
Napoleon, like the soul of Atlantis, is a
"magic."

Our civilization is threatened with destruction through our over-abuse of the "mechanical"; the Atlantes met their doom through an
over-abuse of "magic." Our ways are not their
ways, but our goal is one and the same: a

[54] Taine.
[55] Tyutchev, 1853.
[56] Taine.

titanic dominion over the forces of nature with as its supreme apex, man becoming God. The Atlantes, according to Plato's myth, were "the sons of god." "When through constant inter-mingling with the human nature of mankind, the divine nature in men was exhausted and the human nature became dominant, men became completely depraved. . . . The wise among them saw that men had become evil-minded, but the foolish thought that they had reached to the summits of virtue and happiness, whereas they became possessed with an insane lust for wealth and power. . . . Then it was, that Zeus decided to punish the depraved human race. . . ." And Atlantis disappeared beneath the waves.

It was their titanesque magnitude which caused the fall of the Atlantes, as also that of Napoleon. He above all men was endowed with a sense of divine measure; yet having attained to the summit of power he lost it, or sacrificed it to his titanesque immeasurableness. . . .

What is "Atlantis"? A legend or a prophecy? A past or a future? Why is it that now, as never before, are we conscious of some irresistible reality underlying the "myth?"

"Man will exalt himself with the spirit of *divine* titanic pride, and the man-god will

countenance. The spoken word perhaps would be more likely to capture its elusive traits if only there existed an Orpheus to this Dionysos.

Here is one of the best descriptions of him made by a woman who first almost fell in love with him and afterwards feared and hated him.[1] "Napoleon Bonaparte is of low stature, and ill-made; the upper part of his body is too long in proportion to his legs. He has thin chestnut hair, his eyes are greyish blue, and his skin which was yellow whilst he was slight, has become of late years a dead white without any colour. His forehead, the setting of his eye, the line of his nose—are all beautiful, and remind one of an antique medallion; his mouth, which is thin-lipped, becomes pleasant when he laughs; the teeth are regular; his chin is short, and his jaw heavy and square; he has well-formed hands and feet, I mention them particularly because he thought a good deal of them. . . .

"His eyes are dull, giving to his face a melancholy and meditative expression when in repose. When he is angry he looks fierce and menacing. Laughter becomes him; it makes him look more youthful and less formidable, his countenance improves . . . there was fasci-

[1] Rémusat, I.

nation in the smile of Bonaparte which it was difficult to resist."

Yet even this, the best picture of him, is but an ember in lieu of flame. It lacks the essential, that which caused the dauntless General Vandamme to "tremble like a child each time he approached Napoleon," and which could compel him "to pass through a needle's eye, to throw himself into the fire" for the Emperor.

This feeling is much better expressed in the naïve words of a Belgian peasant, who was Napoleon's guide on the field of Waterloo. When asked what he thought of the Emperor, he replied briefly and enigmatically: "Were his face the dial of a clock, one wouldn't dare to look at the time." (*"Son visage aurait été un cadran d'horloge qu'on n'aurait pas osé regarder l'heure."*) [2]

Here is something still more enigmatic.

The ancients gave much thought to the dual, masculine-feminine nature of the gods: even Apollo Pythian, that most virile of the gods, reveals traits of womanliness, which reaches its climax in Dionysos, the suffering god-son of the Eleussinian mysteries. In his myth Plato recalls how, to curb the excesses of the first dual-

[2] Houssaye, *1815*, II.

natured human beings, the gods divided each of
them in two halves, man and woman, "even as
eggs, when about to be pickled, are cut in half
with a hair." ("The Feast.") Although there is
no allusion to this in the myth, one cannot help
wondering whether the titanic might of the
Atlantes was not the outcome of such a dual
nature.

"He has a certain *embonpoint* which does
not belong to our sex," remarks Las Cases,[3] all
unsuspecting of what mysterious depths in
Napoleon's nature he touches upon. The feminine traits suddenly appear in this most virile
of men not only in the body but in the spirit.
"He is weaker and more sensitive than people
think," says the Empress Josephine who was
familiar with these feminine traits of his.[4] He
himself said: "People often exalted my strength
of character, but I was limp as a rag, particularly with my relatives, who always took advantage of it. My first outburst of anger once
past, they always managed to get the best of me
by their obstinacy and perseverance."[5]

Often he weeps like a woman or has to be
relieved from sudden faintness by sips of

[3] *Memorial,* I.
[4] Lévy.
[5] Lacour-Gayet.

sugared water flavoured with orange blossom like a veritable *marquise* of the eighteenth century.[6] "See, doctor," he says one day to Dr. Antommarchi at St. Helena, emerging quite naked after his morning rub of eau de cologne, "see, what beautiful arms, what rounded breasts, what a smooth white hairless skin. . . . Any beauty might envy such a torso!"[7]

Had anyone told him that the supreme and most formidable of his ideas—that of becoming like the conqueror of India Alexander the Great "a second Dionysos"—the most womanlike of all the gods, was in some mystical way connected with his "*embonpoint* which does not belong to our sex," he would scoff at it and fail to understand. But had that old Austrian who was up to all his "tricks" and "magic," heard the following story he would probably consider it no laughing matter. An old servant just brought over from the country was asked how he liked the new Empress (Marie-Louise) whose triumphant entry in a gold coach drawn by eight horses he had just witnessed. "Oh, she's very beautiful, very!" he replied warmly; "and kind too! Fancy taking her old governess in the carriage with her!" Who that "governess"

Good or Evil?

actually was, was realized only after he described that she had a rotund and very pale face, and wore a crimson velvet toque with long white ostrich plumes—the ceremonial headgear of the Emperor himself—for it was he.[8]

One has but to picture that the "old governess" has eyes like those of a magician "piercing through one's brain," and a countenance, which "were it the dial of a clock one wouldn't dare to look at the time," in order to realize the terror of the poor Austrian: "another of his *tricks,* damn that wizard, now he's turned himself into a woman!"

What is he after all, a "miracle" or a "monster"? What being, "without parallel," divine or demoniac, good or evil, is incarnate in Napoleon?

Nietzsche might perhaps have answered this question as did Mme. de Staël: "neither good nor bad," but on the other side of good and evil. However, such a testimony is too evasive for "on the other side" of human good and evil, there exists the "superhuman" and divine. Besides our puny wooden yard measure of moral values, there is the "golden reed" with which the Angel measures the wall of the City of God

[8] Ch. de Clary, *Trois mois à Paris,* ed. 1914.

"according to the measure of a man, that is, of the angel." And according to that measure, what is Napoleon?

To know this is of the utmost importance to us, for if he, our last hero, is a "monster," then what are we? For as the Man, the Hero is, such too is humanity.

"Bonaparte has an innate evil nature, an innate taste for evil in great things as in small." "It seems as if all magnanimous or manly feelings were alien to him." "This man destroyed every virtue," says the same Mme. de Rémusat, at once infatuated with and hating Bonaparte.[9]

"Far from being cruel Napoleon was kind-hearted by nature," says his last secretary, Baron Fain, himself a simple, kindly man, full of an equally simple affection for Napoleon.[10] This is confirmed by Bourrienne, his first secretary and old school fellow, who was neither kindly nor fond of Napoleon: "I think my judgment of him is sufficiently severe for my verdict to carry weight; and it is I who tell you, politics excepted, he was sensitive, warm-hearted and compassionate."[11] The Emperor of Russia, Alexander I, Napoleon's whilom friend and

[9] Rémusat, I, II and III.
[10] Fain, *Mémoires,* ed. 1909.
[11] Bourrienne, II.

Good or Evil?

future enemy, contributes his testimony in
1810: "People do not know him and judge him
too harshly, perhaps even unjustly. . . . When I
knew him better, I realized he was a good
man." [12]

"*O Napolione!* There is nothing modern in
you, you are a man from Plutarch!" exclaimed
the veteran Corsican hero, Paoli, after a glance
at the nineteen-year-old Bonaparte.[13] "A man
from Plutarch," which means cast in antique
bronze or marble, the perfect hero, a man of
consummate virtue. A few years later, when
the lion cub has shown his claws, that same
Paoli cries out: "see you this little man? He is
two Mariuses and one Sulla combined!" [14] *i.e.,*
a compound of two bandits and one usurper.

Yes, it is difficult to weigh the good and evil
in Napoleon not only by lip evidence but even
by that of the silent feelings of men. "Everyone
loved me and everyone hated." Too dazzling
for human eyes was the interplay of the rays
of love and hatred upon his face.

Here is his own testimony in the nature of a
spontaneous confession made eye to eye to his
evil spirit and tempter, Talleyrand, shortly after

[12] Vandal, *Napoléon et Alexandre,* I, II.
[13] *Memorial,* I.
[14] Chuquet, III.

the terrible Leipzig disaster of 1814. They were discussing what was to be done with Ferdinand VII, the King of Spain, whom "like regular bandits" they had trapped in the French fortress of Bayonne and forced to abdicate in favour of the Emperor of the French. This had led to that guerrilla war with Spain, hopeless, interminable, disastrous and which became one of the causes of Napoleon's fall. Talleyrand, the chief instigator and adviser in this evil deed, now when it was too late, counselled Napoleon to rectify the error by releasing Ferdinand and withdrawing the French troops from Spain.

"You are still too strong for it to be regarded as a cowardly act," he added ambiguously. "A cowardly act?" retorted Napoleon, "what does that matter to me? Understand that I should not fail to commit one if it were useful to me. In reality there is nothing really noble or base in this world. I have in my character all that can contribute to secure my power and to deceive those who think they know me. Frankly, I am base, essentially base. (*'Je suis lâche, essentiellement lâche'*). I give you my word, that I should feel no repugnance to commit what would be called by the world "a dishonourable action." My secret tendencies, which are after all those of nature, apart from certain affectations of greatness which I have to assume, give me infinite resources with which to baffle everyone. Therefore, all I have to do now is to consider whether your advice agrees with my present policy and to try and find out besides," added he with a satanic smile,—"whether you have not some private interest in urging me to take such a step." [15]

To understand this strange confession, one must first understand the confessor. In his own sphere Talleyrand is also an exceptional being: a man of powerful intellect, though absolutely void and dead, for all live intelligence is rooted in the heart, whereas what took the place of Talleyrand's heart was a pinch of grave dust or of the powder of a decayed puff-ball. He is conscious of this bottomless inner void in himself and because of it is fiercely, hungrily jealous of all living beings, of Napoleon in particular, as being essentially "that which is," and "alive."

What binds them together? That quality in Talleyrand which to Napoleon appears as the other's business-like realism, a lack of fastidiousness with regard to the most stinking of all

[15] Rémusat, I.

human laboratories—called politics. Yes, all
that, and something more, of a deeper and more
transcendental nature. They seem to be bound
together like Faust and Mephistopheles, like
man and his shadow "from the other side": the
essentially "un-real" joined to the essentially
"real."

And most surprising of all: at times it seems
as if Napoleon actually loves, or more amazing
still, pitied Talleyrand. Out of some strange
transcendental courtesy or circumspection he
treats this "evil spirit" of his as a guardian
angel. How otherwise to explain the following
incident? Eight years previous to this strange
confession, when Napoleon was leaving Paris
to take the field against Prussia in 1806, he bade
farewell at the Tuileries to both the Empress
Josephine and Talleyrand. He pressed them together tenderly to his heart and wept at having
"to leave the two persons he loved best in the
world!" He was so overcome that he felt faint
and had to be revived with water diluted with
fleur d'oranger.[16]

This momentary infatuation passed, he realized the kind of man he was pitted against, but
even then he was unable to part from him, just

[16] Rémusat, III.

as Faust from Mephistopheles, with the sole
difference that in this case the "magic" per-
tained not to the "shadow" but to the man.

"You are rubbish hidden in a silk bag, sir!"
This is but a specimen of the innumerable light
kicks administered to this over-affectionate
poodle—Mephistopheles. And here is a regular "knock-out" blow.

The scene is enacted in 1809 in the throne
room at the palace of Tuileries in the presence
of high dignitaries of the court after the Emperor's hasty return to Paris from Spain where
he learnt of Talleyrand's conspiracy against
him.

Napoleon storms against Talleyrand in an
access of genuine wrath—a rare occurrence
with him—while the latter, leaning against the
mantelpiece to ease his lame foot—for he is
club-footed, like the devil—listens calmly, receiving the strokes of the lash without so much
as wincing. "You, sir, are a thief and a scoundrel, a man without a conscience for whom
nothing is sacred! All your life long you did
nothing but deceive and betray everyone. You
would sell your own father. I have showered
benefactions on you and yet there is nothing
that you would refuse to do against me. For

ten months past you have been criticizing the trend of my affairs in Spain and have the effrontery to tell all and sundry that you always warned me against that venture, whereas it was you who advised to it. . . . What are your schemes? What is it you hope for? Will you have the effrontery to tell it to my face? You deserve that I should break you like this glass, but I despise you too much to soil myself with such as you!" Neither did he. Talleyrand was not only left unpunished but was soon summoned "to take part in the deliberations of the Council on matters of supreme national importance." [17] That this would be so he was already aware of at the time of Napoleon's outburst, and all the darts of the Emperor's wrath passed not by but through him as if he were a phantom materialized. In this formidable contest, it is difficult to pronounce as to which of the two protagonists was the most powerful and awe-inspiring, the most *"immortal,"* each in his own way, Napoleon or Talleyrand,—the one who "is" or the one who "is not."

What a confession and to what a confessor! Can one believe it? Yes. Talleyrand is far too clever to indulge in crude lies. He is too well

[17] Pasquier, I.

Good or Evil?

aware that crude falsehood is soon divulged
whereas his object is that truth should never
come out, and that the great man should go
down to posterity indelibly branded—by himself—as a "knave." Talleyrand spins a gos-
samer web of truly "satanic" lies which are
"almost truth" and separated from actual truth
by a mere hairbreadth. It is more than likely
that his rendering of Napoleon's words is as
correct as possible; he merely shifts their meaning ever so slightly and thus alters their tone,
their "music." In such counterpoints of falsehood Talleyrand's genius is unrivalled.

Could Napoleon have said: "I am base, fun-
damentally base"? If he did, it was certainly
not with the intention—implied by Talleyrand
—of cynically boasting of his "baseness," of
baring his soul before *such* a mirror. Is there
any scoundrel on earth likely to proclaim his
own baseness? What scoundrel but will lack
the brains to preserve an aspect of nobleness,
and the baser he is, the nobler his demeanour?

Oh, doubtless, Napoleon sweeps away in contempt the moral judgment pronounced on him
by Talleyrand and such as he, with all their
"civilization," like "rubbish in a silk bag."
"My secret inclinations come after all from

nature (*qui viennent de la nature*)." . . . With all his genius for falsehood, Talleyrand would be incapable to invent *that*: here it is the voice of Napoleon speaking, the roar of the "prehistoric monster." Probably genuine too is the statement: "after all there is nothing in the world that is really noble or base." He should have added: "in your world, Monsieur de Talleyrand." Is not that for Talleyrand an absolute truth? Whose image then was reflected in that truth as in a mirror—Napoleon's or that of Talleyrand himself?

It seems as if this time, this genius of imposture was himself made to play the fool, and, what is more, appears to have foreseen it should be so. He complains to his *confidante,* Mme. de Rémusat: "This devil of a man fools us all, even about his passions, for he knows how to act them, though he does actually possess them." [18] What they are would appear sufficiently obvious: ambition, love of power? No. Talleyrand knows or premises vaguely that the object of Napoleon's real passions, or rather of his one and only ruling passion is something deeper, more elemental. What is it then? He does not know. Neither do we, or at any rate we

[18] Rémusat, I.

are unable to give it its proper name, and can only surmise it. It is the *fulness of being,*—not life, but that from which all life proceeds and to which it returns,—*being* in its supreme consummation. It is that state of "being" which according to Nietzsche, makes of Napoleon "the most real of all creatures,—*ens realissimum*" and which is least accessible to Talleyrand as the man who essentially "is not." Such is the object of Napoleon's sole and dominating passion, and that is why Talleyrand's jealous hatred of him is so quenchless and impotent.

If in spite of everything, even his "evil genius," a "slanderer" *par excellence* fails to discover in him that fundamental evil which justifies a man being branded as a "villain," where then is his villainy?

"A fall usually has the effect of lowering a man's character, but on the contrary my fall has elevated me prodigiously," says Napoleon at St. Helena. "Every succeeding day divests me of some portion of my tyrant's skin." [19] How did it grow on him? Has not he in the course of his life-time committed at least one absolutely evil deed—one crime?

He appears to believe in all sincerity that he

[19] *Memorial,* IV.

has not. "Crime is alien to my nature.[20] I rose
. . . to the astonishing height of power I possessed without having committed a single crime
to obtain it. At my last hour I can assert that
I never committed a crime. . . . Had I done
so, I should not have been here now." (St.
Helena). "I am too much of a fatalist, and have
too great a contempt for human nature."[21]

What about the affair of the Duc d'Enghien?
Has he forgotten it, or does he remember, but
considers himself not guilty?

The case was this. At the beginning of 1804,
forty conspirators, mainly in the pay of the
English government, were arrested on the
charge of conspiring against the life of the
First Consul. Among them were Georges
Cadoudal, a Breton *chouan* (royalist) and Generals Pichegru and Moreau, the latter Bonaparte's erstwhile rival and famous victor of
Hohenlinden. Since the attempt on his life
made three years before at the rue Nikèze, assassins swarmed around the person of the First
Consul. "The air is thick with daggers," the
Minister of Police Fouché warned him.[22] He
himself knew this. "Am I a dog that I should be

[20] *Memorial*, IV.
[21] O'Meara, I.
[22] Lacour-Gayet.

killed in the street?" [23] "I had a natural right to self-defence, I was attacked at all times and from every side . . . air-muskets, infernal machines, plots, ambuscades of every sort. . . . Finally I grew tired of it and took the opportunity of carrying the terror across the Channel . . . War for War . . . blood for blood. . . ." "After all, my own blood is not mud. My great rule is that in war and in politics evil is justifiable in so far as it is a necessity; otherwise it is a crime," [24] he says at St. Helena.

It was supposed—mistakenly as was subsequently proved—that Louis Bourbon Condé Duc d'Enghien and one of the last scions of the ancient royal house of France, took part in the conspiracy and had even sojourned for a time in Paris. A sickly looking man of about thirty, with the pale and melancholy countenance of a "disconsolate knight," he lived a solitary life at Ettenheim, a small town in the duchy of Baden close to the Rhine and the French border, taking no part in politics, and dividing his time between hunting and love dreams.

"I can recall it, as if it were but yesterday," Napoleon continues his reminiscences at St. Helena: "I was having my after-dinner coffee,

[23] Ségur, II.
[24] *Memorial,* IV.

when they came in and announced the discovery
of a conspiracy by the Duc d'Enghien. . . . I
did not even quite know who he was. . . . But
it was all pre-arranged." [25] It was the work of
Talleyrand. It was he too who insisted on the
duke being arrested on foreign territory in
direct violation of international law.

On the 15th of March a platoon of French
gendarmes, armed with swords and pistols,
crossed the frontier, entered Ettenheim and in
silence surrounded the duke's house, which they
broke into. The duke was seized, shuffled into
a closed carriage and brought first to Stras-
burg and thence, under escort, to Paris, where
he was imprisoned in the fortress of Vincennes.
The First Consul wished to entrust the investi-
gation of the case to General Murat, then governor of the city of Paris, but he refused point-
blank. "They want to besmirch my uniform,
but this I will not allow!" [26] Bonaparte then
took the whole responsibility upon himself,
though of course his "guardian angel"—Talleyrand—was the actual wire-puller. Savary, the
Minister of Police, was but a blind instrument
in the hands of both.

A court-martial commission was appointed

[25] *Memorial,* IV.
[26] Pasquier, I.

for the duke's trial. "Everything to be finished
to-night," so the order ran. "If, as I have no
doubt, the verdict will be sentence of death, it is
to be carried out immediately, and the criminal
to be interred in one of the fortress courts.—
Bonaparte."[27]

The duke's absolute innocence was proved at
the very first examination. "I urgently request
a personal interview with the First Consul. My
name, my rank, my disposition and the horror
of my situation—all lead me to hope that my
request will be granted."[28] wrote the duke at
the end of his questionnaire.

This request did not reach Bonaparte: it was
intercepted by Talleyrand.

At two o'clock in the morning on the 21st
of March the duke was again brought before
the commission. The second examination added
nothing to the evidence in hand. The accused
bore himself with great dignity, made no attempt to conceal—what was common knowledge—his readiness to join the armies of the
powers at war against the illegal government
of Bonaparte, "as befits my rank and the blood
flowing in my veins"; but he indignantly repudiated the very idea of his participation in

[27] Lacour-Gayet.
[28] *Ibid.*

an attempt against the life of the First Consul.
No sooner was the prisoner led away, than the
judges passed the sentence of death, and being
ignorant in conformity with what points of law
he was being judged, left a blank space in the
verdict. The duke's innocence was so obvious
that the judges decided to add a petition of
their own to the duke's appeal to the First Consul. It came too late.[29]

At half-past two in the morning—the trial
had lasted less than half an hour—the gendarmes entered the duke's cell. As he was being
led down the steps into the moat, he asked where
they were going. No one answered. A rush of
cold air came from below. He seized one of the
men by the arm and again asked: "To prison?"
Then suddenly he saw the firing party and
understood. He cut off a lock of hair, which together with his ring he asked to be sent to his
beloved, the Princess de Rohan-Rochefort. He
asked: "May I not have a priest?" "Does he
want to die a *capucin*?" sounded somebody's
mocking voice from the rampart—it was that of
the Minister, Savary. The duke knelt down,
said a prayer, then rose and said: "How terrible to die by the hand of Frenchmen!" He re-

[29] Pasquier, I.

134

fused to be blindfolded. The volley rang out, and he fell dead.[30]

All the previous day the First Consul spent locked up in his study. Josephine rushed to him in tears, fell at his feet and implored him to save the duke. He pushed her away roughly with his foot, saying: "Go away! You are a child and know nothing of politics!"

At five in the morning, as he lay in bed beside her, he woke her up and said: "the Duc d'Enghien is already dead." She screamed and burst into tears. "Never mind, sleep!" he told her sharply, adding as before: "you child!" [31]

Was this callousness? Scarcely that. Two days before the execution Chateaubriand saw the First Consul at a levée at the Tuileries. The expression of his face was so terrible that on his return home the poet told his friends: "Bonaparte is either ill, or something unusual has happened of which we are ignorant." [32]

"Oh, *mon ami,* what have you done!" wept Josephine on the day of the execution. "Yes, these unfortunate men have made a mess of it," he replied thoughtfully, then added: "Well, it can't be helped now, I must take the blame on myself: to lay it on others would be mean." [33]

[30] Lacour-Gayet.   [32] Lacour-Gayet.
[31] Pasquier.   [33] Ségur, II.

Count de Ségur saw him three or four days
later at mass in the chapel of the Tuileries. "I
watched him closely . . . the blood-stained
shadow of his victim seemed to rise before the
altar. . . . I sought to detect in his countenance
the traces of remorse or leastways of regret . . .
yet nothing was changed on that face . . . it was
calm and inscrutable."

After mass the First Consul walked among
the assembled statesmen and spoke to them of
the trial of the Duc d'Enghien, obviously de-
sirous to learn the impression it had created.
But the only responses were either servile flat-
tery or grim silence. And suddenly he too became sternly silent, turned on his heel and
abruptly left the room.[34]

"We are replunged into the atrocities of '93
by the very hand which drew us out of them,"
said Count de Ségur, voicing the feelings of the
best men of his day. "I was overwhelmed . . .
I used to be proud of the great man whom I
served; to me he embodied the type of the perfect hero, whereas now . . ." He lacks the courage to add: "now the hero is turned into a
criminal."

Shortly after Bonaparte reaped the reward

[34] Ségur, II.

of the murder—three and a half million votes in favour of the Senate's proposal to proclaim him Emperor—he stepped on to the throne over the still warm body of Enghien.

Thus once again was accomplished the ancient horror of Gorgon: the priest stabbed the heart of the victim and "beheld the sun in all its glorious splendour!"

"These people wanted to destroy the Revolution by destroying me," the Emperor tells his attendants: "It was my duty both to defend and to avenge the Revolution. I have proved of what it is capable!" "When calm is restored, people will cease to accuse me—they will realize that this execution was a great political necessity." "Once and for all I have silenced both Jacobins and Royalists." [35]

"There, Sire, do not let us speak of it, or you will make me cry," . . . Mme. de Rémusat said to him once, when the conversation turned to the duke. He laughed: "Ah! tears! Woman's only weapon!" [36]

Most terrible of all is that he appears not to grasp the significance of this act. A child would understand, whereas he, the most intelligent of men, fails.

[35] Rémusat, I.
[36] *Ibid.*

"How? Do they still harp on that old story? What childishness!" He appears genuinely surprised to learn that the affair of the Duc d'Enghien is well remembered in Petersburg.[37]

Yet, he himself remembers him only too well and the further the event recedes, the more vivid his remembrance of it. . . . How much blood was shed by him, and forgotten, but not this. . . .

It cannot be said that he never repented of, or leastways acknowledged his evil deeds. "I have made a bad mess of this affair," he says of the seizure of the Spanish throne, which led to that interminable war in which he became involved as in a quagmire and never got out of again. "Its immorality was too blatant, the injustice too cynical, and because I failed everything assumed a much more sinister aspect. . . . This canker has eaten into me." And again referring to other things: "One cannot lie upon the bed of kings without becoming infected with their madness; so it is with me." [38]

He confesses all his evil deeds, but of this,

[37] Rémusat, III.
[38] Lacour-Gayet.

the blackest of them all, he is unrepentant; for so at least it appears to him and to others.

Las Cases at St. Helena dares not mention the Duc d'Enghien and blushes when Napoleon himself speaks of him "with calm, irrefutable and convincing logic." "When he finished, I was struck dumb with amazement. . . . I am convinced he would now have pardoned him." Thus in confidential talk, but before strangers "he would suddenly change his tone and say that he regretted the turn the affair had taken, but felt neither repentance nor any scruples for what he had done." [39]

Nevertheless his conscience is divided on that point. "That *scelerato* Talleyrand did not make it (the duke's letter) known until two days after his execution." [40] Had he done so earlier: "I should certainly have pardoned him," he says once; and then, "as if addressing posterity": "were it necessary to do this over again, I should have done so." [41] He himself is uncertain as to what he ought to have done—pardoned or condemned.

Three days before the end, in the throes of the death agony, he ordered the sealed envelope

[39] *Memorial,* IV.
[40] O'Meara, I.
[41] *Memorial,* IV.

containing his testament to be brought to him, opened it, added something to the writing, sealed it up again and returned the envelope to his attendants. This is what he wrote: "I had the Duc d'Enghien arrested and tried because that step was essential to the safety, interest and the honour of the French people, when the Comte d'Artois was maintaining by his confession sixty assassins at Paris. Under similar circumstances I would again act in the same way." [42]

Does not this signify: "Before the face of death, before the face of God, I am not guilty"? Yes, indeed; but also something more, and quite different.

"Whatever he may have said to the contrary, I believe in his remorse: it pursued him to the grave. It was this racking self-reproach that forced him to add these words to his testament," says chancellor Pasquier who knew Napoleon well and was a close witness of the whole affair.[43] He is probably right. All his life long Napoleon was tortured by that memory, it haunted him at his death bed,—remorse without repentance.

The simplest and most equitable judgment

[42] *Memorial,* IV.
[43] Pasquier, I.

on the deed was passed by Lord Holland, a true friend of Napoleon: "A crime is not to be palliated, much less justified by its consequences . . . and the sacrifice of this man . . . will and ought to remain a blot on his memory." [44] But were the question put: "Napoleon committed a villainy; therefore he is a villain?" Lord Holland's answer, like that of his entire book would be: "no, a good man."

Can a good man commit "villainies"? Before answering, let each one of us ask himself, whether in our own life there is not an "Enghien"? It may be that, not the worst but the best of us will reply: "yes, there is." . . . Yes, each of us has his *own Enghien*—the plague spot, by which is revealed in every soul that which is known to Christians as the "original sin." With small men that spot is small, with average of average size, that of big men, large as themselves.

Meek King David had it too: the blood of Uriah the Hittite. Though the difference between King David and Napoleon is certainly great: the former repented, whereas the latter either refused or was unable to repent, or perhaps was himself unaware of his repentance.

[44] Lord Holland.

"Everyone loved and everyone hated me, . . ."
And none pitied. . . . And yet perhaps it was
what he needed most because, however strange
it may seem, he deserved compassion in spite
of all his grandeur. To realize this, it is but
sufficient to remember, that the least among
men can pray, whereas he could not.

Nevertheless, he is a "good man." Poor
Toby, the old Malay slave on St. Helena, knows
this. How Napoleon wished to pay his ransom,
but the governor of the island, Hudson Lowe,
forbade it. Napoleon pitied poor Toby perhaps
because he sensed something similar in their
destinies: both were victims of European
"civilization." Toby was a freeborn savage;
Europeans "civilized" him, lured him from his
native land and sold him into slavery. Toby too
learnt to love Napoleon; spoke of him always
as the "good gentleman," or better still the
"good man." [45]

The plague-stricken soldiers in Jaffe know
it too. During the campaign in Syria, young
General Bonaparte on the 11th of March, 1799,
visited the plague hospital, and wishing to set
an example to the panic-stricken doctors and
calm the soldiers by proving that plague was

[45] O'Meara, I. *Memorial,* I. Abbell (Betsy Balcombe).

not as dangerous as reputed, he spent a long time among the sick, chatted to and soothed them, held their hands and helped to carry one of them.[46]

The wounded know it too. Those wounded, for whose use all the horses, his own included, mules and camels were abandoned by order of the general during the ghastly retreat from Acre across the scorching Syrian desert. When his equerry, disbelieving the order, asks which horse to saddle, Bonaparte strikes him across the face with his whip and shouts: "Everyone on foot, damn you, and myself first of all."

Those French peasants too know it who on that last journey of his from Niort to Roche-fort and on to St. Helena run after his carriage weeping and shouting: *"Vive l'Empereur!* Stay, stay with us." It was haymaking time, and the tall hay-ricks reminded them of the vast drainage work carried out by Napoleon's order in 1807 and which had con verted the sterile, marshy, fever-infested plain into flowering meadowland. "See how grateful the people are to me for the good I have done them!" he says to his fellow travellers.[47] Yes,

[46] Contrary to Bourrienne's opinion (I.) this is confirmed not only by Count Dor, Dr. Larrey, Dr. Jennet, but by Napoleon himself in his conversation with O'Meara (III).
[47] Houssaye, *1815,* III.

everything will pass away and be forgotten, but this will remain—a drained marsh, "chaos rebuilt."

They know it too, those thousands who with a cry of rapture, *"Vive l'Empereur!"* die for him on the fields of battle. They know or feel that he strives for good, this man whose supreme aim—the universal unity of mankind—is also the supreme good.

"Napoleon lived wholly for ideas, but was nevertheless unable to grasp the nature of ideal motives," again and again one recalls Goethe's words of wisdom. "He repudiated the ideal, denied there was any such thing . . . and himself was eagerly trying to realize the ideal." This means: words and thoughts may be evil, but the will to do—is good. He is a better man than he makes himself out to be: the evil is on the surface, the good inside.

He should not be judged by the expression of that immovable, inexorable countenance as if cast in bronze or marble. "I might hear of the death of my wife, son and all my kin without moving a muscle; my expression would remain indifferent and unfeeling. It is only when I am alone that I become human and I suffer." [48]

[48] O'Meara, II.

Good or Evil?

Diffidence in showing suffering, diffidence in showing goodness—which generally go together—are his in a supreme degree. "There are two men in me: one is of the head, the other of the heart." [49] "Do not think me more unfeeling than other people. I am even kind-hearted, but from early infancy I strove to suppress this part of my nature, and now it is stifled." [50] Did he himself suppress it, or was it life which did it? In the toil and moil of life his soul became hardened like the hands of the labourer, but not stifled.

"His first care, after a battle, was for the wounded"—writes Baron Fain. "He would himself walk over the field, and order them to be picked up, friend and foe alike; himself would see to it that their wounds should be dressed, and that all to the last man should be carried to the dressing stations or nearest hospitals."—"Some he would specially confide to the care of his court surgeon Ivan, and he would follow every detail of the case, questioning as to the nature of the wound, of the chance of recovery, the amount of danger. Many a good deed—God alone knows how many—was thus done in secret. "His campaign purse

[49] Roederer.
[50] Fournier, III.

145

seemed to have a hole in it, so generously did his largesse flow from it." [51]

On the battlefield of Borodino Napleon's horse stumbled over a wounded man; he moved with a groan. The Emperor in a rage railed at his staff officers, blaming them for neglect of the wounded. "But this is a Russian, Sire," some-one said to pacify him. "What of that?" he shouted still more angrily: "don't you know, sir, that there are no more enemies after vic-tory—all are men." [52]

Walking over the battlefield of Ligny, two days before Waterloo, he came upon a badly wounded Prussian officer. He motioned to a Belgian peasant to approach. "Do you believe in hell?" "I do."—"Then if you don't want to go to hell, look after this wounded man, I leave him in your care. Otherwise you will burn in hell: God desires us all to be merciful." [53] This is not a prayer, but is perhaps worth many.

One day at St. Helena he recalled how after some big battle during the first campaign in Italy—twenty years before—he was with a few companions making his usual survey of the field, still strewn with the bodies of the slain.

[51] Fain.
[52] Ségur, IV.
[53] Houssaye, *1815*, II.

Good or Evil?

It was a calm moonlit night, and suddenly they came upon a dog howling over the dead body of its master. It ran up to them as they approached; then it ran back to the corpse and licked the dead face, then back to them again, and so backwards and forwards howling all the time, "as if asking for an avenger or begging for help." "No incident on any field of battle ever produced so deep an impression on me. This man, thought I, lies here forsaken by all except his dog! What a lesson Nature here presents through the medium of an animal! Such is man, and what secret is concealed in his moods! I had beheld with tearless eyes the execution of those operations by which thousands of my countrymen were sacrificed, and here my feelings were roused by the howling of a dog!" [54]

He himself howls like a dog, or like Achilles over Patrocles, over Marshal Lennes, the bravest of the brave, when both his legs were torn away by a shell in the battle of Essling. That night, alone in his tent, when supper is brought to him he forced himself to eat, and tears fell in his soup. [55]

"What a terrible sight!" he repeats over and

[54] *Memorial,* I.
[55] Marbot., II. Ségur, III. *Memorial,* III.

power, a statesman never looks at persons, he only takes account of phenomena, their value and effects." "He seems as though he could be equally capable of becoming the ally of his most cruel enemy, and of living with the man who did him the greatest wrong," is Las Cases' wondering comment.

Napoleon himself attributed the ease with which he forgave men solely to his contempt for them, but perhaps this was not the only reason.

"You do not know men," he would tell his fellow-captives on St. Helena when they gave vent to their indignation against those who betrayed him: "It is difficult to give people their due. . . . Do they even know themselves? As a matter of fact I was more forsaken rather than betrayed, there was more weakness than perfidy about me. It was the denial of St. Peter; tears and repentance are probably at hand." And he concluded with what is perhaps his wisest and most magnanimous saying: "After all, most people are not really bad." [61]

Our "Christian" civilization does not possess a word for defining what was known to the ancients as *virtus*. This is not our *virtue,* but

[61] *Memorial,* IV.

rather valour, virility, and withal kindness of heart, as expressive of the supreme force and firmness of character. Of this nature was Napoleon's kindliness. Upon this "holy rock"— *Pietra-Santa,* as one of his Corsican great-grandmothers was named—his whole personality was built.

Gratitude—that ever-burning remembrance of good once received, that steadfast adherence to good, is essentially a manly virtue, and that is why it is so prominent in Napoleon.

"I despise ingratitude as the basest vice the human heart is capable of," are his words coming straight from the depth of his own heart. Gratitude is goodness concealed, the warmth of very deep waters. Diffidently he denies it in himself: "I am not kind, oh no, I never was kind-hearted, but I am trustworthy." (*"Je ne suis pas bon, non, je ne l'ai jamas été, mais je suis sur"*).[62]

Napoleon's testament is one of the most magnificent and edifying memorials of human "trustworthiness."

No one who ever did him a kindness is forgotten. Himself, a dying man, he recalls to life all those, long since dead, to whom he considers

[62] Lord Holland.

himself indebted. He shows his gratitude to them in the persons of their children and grandchildren, and is always afraid lest someone be forgotten. Ten days before the end, racked by intolerable pain, he nevertheless writes with his own hand a fourth codicil to his will, "because some of our obligations were left unfulfilled in the previous clauses." Follow thirteen fresh items: "To the son or grandson of General Dugomier, who commanded the army of Toulon, the sum of 100,000 francs . . . it is a testimonial of remembrance for the marks of esteem, of respect, affection and of friendship, which that brave and intrepid general gave to us. One-hundred thousand francs to the son or grandson of the Deputy of the Convention, Gasparin, for having perfected and sanctioned with his authority the plan which we had given for the siege of Toulon. One-hundred thousand francs to the widow, son or grandson of our aide-de-camp, Muiron, killed at our side at Arcola, covering us with his body."

One of the very first clauses mentions: One-hundred thousand francs to Larrey, the surgeon-in-chief, "the most virtuous man I have ever known." [63] Goodness recognizes goodness.

[63] *Memorial*, IV.

Good or Evil?

That all his life long he should provide for his old nurse Camilla Clary, the wife of a poor Corsican fisherman, is not surprising. More surprising is the pension which he secretly paid from his private casket to the nurse of King Louis XVI and to two destitute old women— the sisters of Maximilien Robespierre,[64] thus by an act of sublime simplicity reconciling in his own heart the executioner with the victim.

It is easier to catch the human heart unawares in small things than in great; a hero is sometimes better discerned in a glimpse through a keyhole than when framed in a triumphal arch.

"I can only speak of him when half-dressed, and like this he was always kind," are the valet Constant's recollections of his master.[65]

It happened once in one of the campaigns on the Rhine that after several sleepless nights Constant fell fast asleep in the tent in the Emperor's own arm chair resting his head and arms on the maps and papers piled on the writing desk. Suddenly Napoleon entered with Marshal Berthier and the Mameluke Roustan. They wanted to wake the sleeper, but the Em-

[64] Fain.
[65] Constant, I.

peror would not let them, and as there was no
other chair in the tent, he sat down on the edge
of his camp bed and continued to give Berthier
his orders concerning next day's operations.
When it became necessary to consult a map,
Napoleon went up to the table and began gently
pulling it from beneath Constant's elbow, trying not to wake him. But the valet jumped up
mumbling apologies.

"I am very sorry I woke you, Monsieur Constant," said Napoleon, with a kindly smile,
"pray forgive me!" [66]

Many of his soldiers' rude jokes—such as
spilling ink over Josephine's pink gown because he disliked it, and even the alleged noto-
rious knee-kick delivered in the stomach of the
philosopher Volney after the latter's foolish
blasphemy—may be forgiven him for this act
of kingly courtesy.

A page in his retinue, a mere boy, was riding
at the door of the Imperial carriage in torren-
tial rain. On leaving the carriage Napoleon saw
that the boy was wet through, ordered him to
stay behind and inquired many times after his
health. The boy wrote of this to his mother,
who, on reading his letter, perhaps learnt some-

[66] Constant, IV.

thing about the Emperor Napoleon of which his forty thousand judges still know nothing.[67]

Doctor O'Meara, at St. Helena, fell in a fainting fit at Napoleon's feet. When he recovered consciousness he saw the Emperor kneeling over him on the floor, and rubbing his temples with eau de cologne. "I shall never forget the countenance of Napoleon, bending over my face and regarding me with an expression of great concern and anxiety," adds O'Meara.[68]

The best that is in people is always the most simple and childlike. "Bad people seldom love children, and Napoleon loved them," writes Bourrienne.[69]

Sitting on the floor, the First Consul plays like a child with his little nephew Napoleon, his face wearing a genial, natural expression. The next moment he assumes a terrible mask to receive the British ambassador, Lord Whitworth, whom he rails at and threatens with breaking off diplomatic relations.[70]

"I spent the last two days with Marshal Bessières; we frolicked with him like boys of fif-

[67] Lévy.
[68] O'Meara, I.
[69] Bourrienne, II.
[70] Rémusat, I.

teen," he wrote in 1806, between Austerlitz and Iena.

Betsy Balcombe, the fourteen-year-old daughter of the owners of the Briars on St. Helena, in whose house Napoleon spent the first months of his exile, was dreadfully afraid to meet him, because almost from her babyhood she had heard him spoken of as a terrible ogre, particularly fond of eating up little girls. But she soon grew fond of him and played with him as if he were of her own age. Many years later, as an old lady, she always spoke of the Emperor as of her erstwhile playmate.[71]

General Gourgaud, one of his voluntary fellow captives at St. Helena, at last resolved to quit the Emperor, but was ashamed to tell him so. As they were walking in the garden one day, Napoleon caught sight of a pin lying on the path, picked it up and handed it to Gourgaud with a childlike smile: "Here, Gourgaud, my little Gourgaud, here is a pin—I make you a present of it." To make a present of any sharp object means a quarrel. That is exactly what Gourgaud does want.[72] It is as if Napoleon had said to him: "That thou doest, do quickly." Sorrow, rebuke, caress, banter, forgiveness—are all

[71] Abell.
[72] Gourgaud, II.

there, and all are childlike. But nothing of this did Gourgaud understand, just as Napoleon's child-nature remains forever incomprehensible to the hopelessly grown-up Taine or to Tolstoy, equally hopelessly yearning after childhood. "Except ye be converted, and become as little children . . ." this means the childlike in man is of God. That is why the hero, Man—God and child dwell together.

Thus are good and evil intermingled in Napoleon. What is he himself—good or bad? To call him absolutely good—a saint—would be as rudely false as to call him a villain. In him good and evil are in perpetual conflict. Yet in this conflict, as in much else, he is a being of a different nature from ours, a creature from another sphere of creation,—"a man from Atlantis." His heart is a chalice filled with a peculiar fluid; a drop of some sacrificial blood, not yet that of Golgotha, has fallen into some kind of ambrosia, not yet Olympian, and has formed that seething blend we call "Napoleon's genius." But only, *we,* the children of the most godless of all ages, are capable of designating him simply as a "villain."

To revile the hero, Man, is to revile mankind. We have been reviling Napoleon for the past hundred years! Has not the time come to say at last: on this of all heroes the most calumny has been heaped.

No human countenance after death could equal in beauty that of Napoleon on his death-bed.[73] Serene and pure as the heaven above, surely that face testifies that in death at least if not in life the good in him had triumphed over the evil and he had indeed fulfilled "the measure of a man, that is, of the angel." A slumbering demi-god and angel combined, a cherubim of light and power, fallen from heaven to earth. . . . But we failed to recognize him, and this is how we served him!

[73] Lacour-Gayet. Abrantès, ed. Albin Michel, III. Napoleon on his death-bed, a sketch by Capt. Marryat made on the 5th May, 1821, day of the Emperor's death.

CHAPTER VI

THE WORKER

A COMBINATION of extremes—such could be the definition of Napoleon's genius; so he defines it himself.

"It is both difficult and unusual to find a combination of all the qualities which go to make a great general. The most desirable combination, which places a man at once into a prominent position, is the equilibrium between mind or talent and character or valour." [1] This, as expressed by Napoleon, is *"to be well squared both by the base and the perpendicular."* The base of the square is will—valour; its perpendicular—intellect.

"In Bonaparte intellect balances the will" (*"La partie intellectuelle balance la volonté"*), is the profound remark of Abbé Sièyes. [2] Such a state of equilibrium between mind and will actually is "a well-squared genius."

We all, the creatures of modern European

[1] *Memorial*, I.
[2] Vandal, *Bonaparte*, I.

civilization, are suffering more or less from Hamlet's disease, the dissociation of the intellect from the will, of contemplation and action. Napoleon alone appears healthy among the sick. Within us all, the two souls—diurnal and nocturnal—are severed asunder; in him alone they are united. We all have tested of the tree of knowledge and are dying; he alone has tested both of the tree of knowledge and of that of life—and lives. We all develop our minds at the expense of our wills; he alone unites illimitable intellect with endless will-power. We all represent squares that are either squat and low—those of will, or tall and narrow—those of the intellect; he alone is the perfect square.

Just as within his being are united two opposing principles,—will-power and intellect, so each of these separately combines opposing qualities within themselves.

Memory and imagination are the first pair of intellectual contrasts; turned towards the future are the dynamics of imagination, looking back into the past are the statics of memory.

"I possess an extraordinary memory. In my youth I knew the logarithms of more than thirty or forty numbers. I not only knew the names of all the officers in all the French regiments but the localities from which the men were conscripted, their military exploits and even the political views of each." [3]

When as an Emperor he used to verify military reports (*états de situation*) dealing with hundreds of thousands of men quartered from Danzig to Gibraltar, he would note the slightest mistake. "Why are fifteen gendarmes on the island of Vlaherne without arms?" "Why two four-inch guns placed in Ostende are not mentioned?" [4] In 1813 he recollects having sent three years since two squadrons of the 20th horse chasseurs to Spain. He knew all the military reports almost by heart, and by his regimental number could have directed a stray soldier to the billets of his corps. [5]

Memory was for him like an inexhaustible quarry from which his imagination extracted the stones for his titanic structure.

"The Emperor is all imagination," remarks de Pradt. [6] One might add: "and all memory," or in general "all" that mental quality which he needed at any particular moment, often a direct contrast to that which he "wholly" was a minute ago. His mind is a many-faced Proteus,

[3] Gourgaud, II.
[4] Lévy.
[5] Abbé de Pradt, Taine.
[6] Abbé de Pradt.

assuming and discarding the guise of all things in turn.

"This cold politician was fired by an extraordinary imagination. His intellect carried out the ideas of a poet. He certainly could not have accomplished what he did had he no Muse to inspire him." [7]

"I sometimes believe that all this strange man's dreams may come true, and with such an imagination who knows what he may be dreaming about," was Josephine's prophetic comment on him after their first meeting. [8]

His imagination made him as great a poet in action as were Aeschylus, Dante and Goethe in contemplation; the conductor of a new universally historic symphony, a new Orpheus whose music compelled stones to range themselves into the walls of the City. "I love power like an artist, as the fiddler loves his fiddle . . . I love power in order to draw from it sounds, melodies and harmonies. . . ." [9] And of all harmonies, the greatest, the universal union of mankind.

Knowledge, as creative action, and knowledge as pure contemplation are another of his

[7] Lacour-Gayet.
[8] *Ibid.*
[9] Roederer.

intellectual contrasts. More than everyone else he is the man to discover the active Archimedes' fulcrum of the will for the lever of knowledge. Yet withal, the joy of pure contemplation is so familiar to him that at times he wonders whether he was not born to be a great savant and had betrayed his true vocation by giving up contemplation for action.

"Here is another opportunity to make me regret having been drawn by force of circumstances so far away from the path of science,"— he wrote to Laplace, thanking him for the dedication in the "Heavenly Mechanics" inscribed to him, and expressing his admiration for its "perfect lucidity." And amid the growing horrors of the year 1812 he does not omit to thank the astronomer for sending to Vitebsk a copy of his "Theory of Probabilities," "a work which is destined to perfect mathematics, the first among all sciences." [10]

Like Pythagoras he hearkens to the mysterious harmonies of the numbers. At times of stress to calm his nerves he reads the tables of the logarithms as though they were a missal. [11]

On the return voyage from Egypt, on board the frigate *Muiron,* while his companions are

[10] Chuquet, I.
[11] Holland.

in a state of constant dread lest they be over-
taken by the British fleet which is in pursuit of
them, General Bonaparte coolly discourses on
chemistry, physics and mathematics with the
members of the Institute, Berthollet and
Monge.[12]

At Malmaison, after his second abdication in
1815, the Emperor tells Monge: "to me inac-
tivity is torture. Bereft of an empire, without
an army, my only resort is in science. . . . I want
to start a new life in order to leave to posterity
the fruits of scientific labours and discoveries
worthy of me. . . . You and I will explore the
New World from Canada to Cape Horn, and
in the course of our travels study all the physical phenomena of our globe." Never had
Monge been so impressed by Napoleon's greatness. But suddenly the distant roar of the cannon smites his ear, and again he hastens to his
maps which he studs with pins; and once
more he dreams of war—action.[13] So unto the
very end and he knows not which is most congenial to him—contemplation or action.

At St. Helena oblivious of his own sufferings
he would spend hours in one of the forsaken
rooms at Longwood, watching the life of ants,

[12] Ségur, I.
[13] Houssaye, *1815*, III.

admiring their instinct and perseverence to find a hidden lump of sugar: "This is intelligence, it is more than instinct, it is real intelligence . . . a model of statesmanship. Oh, if only men were as united!" [14] This wisdom of the ants, like the howling of the dog over the body of its master, are to him evidence that dumb creatures may be nearer to their Creator than human beings.

Already sick unto death, he spends whole days observing the fishes in the fish-pond at Longwood, particularly their love-making and fighting; and when as a consequence of some disease or poisoning they begin to die off, he becomes seriously upset and treats it as a bad omen: "This means that I too am going to die." [15]

When still in good health, he would spend long hours studying Las Cases's planisphere atlas, or hold forth on new geological hypotheses, on the still unknown courses of cyclones and gales, on the continuous air and water currents—these mighty breaths of Mother Earth, which to him as to the ancient Ionic philosophers was no dead block of matter, but the living body of the Great Animal—Zoön.[16] Since

[14] Antommarchi, I.
[15] Ibid.   [16] Memorial, IV.

the days of the ancients never, except perhaps
Goethe's and Leonardo da Vinci's, had the
human heart beat so in unison with the heart of
Mother Earth as did Napoleon's.

> One life he breathed with nature.
> The murmur of the streams he understood
> And how the green leaves whisper on the trees:
> Felt in himself the springing of the grass:
> The book of stars was open to his mind
> And with him spake the waves upon the sea.[17]

Synthesis and analysis are the third of his
intellectual contrasts. Synthesis consummate,
the supreme harmony of Orpheus's harp—power
—is the universal community of nations. The
breadth of this synthesis corresponds to the
depth of the analysis.

"I was always fond of analysis; had I ever
fallen seriously in love, I should have dissected
my feelings. The 'why' and 'wherefore' are
such useful questions, that the oftener they are
put, the better." [18]

"The geometrical structure of his mind compelled him to analyze everything—even his
proper feelings," writes Mme. de Rémusat.
"Bonaparte was a man who always pondered

[17] Baratynsky, *On the Death of Goethe,* trans. by Miss Margot
R. Adamson.
[18] Rémusat, I.

over the motives of men's actions. Always in a
state of moral tension and continually analyz-
ing the secret motives of his own feelings, he
was never able to explain or understand the
natural carefree mentality which at times
prompts us to act without aim or purpose." [19]
The latter comment, however, is incorrect:
though he was certainly alien to the carefree
mentality of society butterflies like Mme. de
Rémusat, it does not follow that Napoleon was
incapable of the spontaneousness and impulse
which are inherent to "nocturnal consciousness"—intuition.

Measure and immeasurableness are the fourth
pair of his intellectual contrasts.

The solar genius of the whole Mediterranean
race, from Pythagoras to Pascal—geometrical
clearness, precision and simplicity which are
the measure of Apollo—is also that of Napoleon's genius. His style according to Sainte-
Beuve recalls that of Pascal; and it should be
added: and that of Pythagoras; "words as if
graven with a pair of compasses." [20]

The chaos of revolution is bridled as it were
by the order of numbers and reduced to geometrical proportions. "Everywhere I intro-

[19] Rémusat, I.
[20] Lévy.

duced uniform simplicity, for all that is good
and beautiful is the outcome of a simple and
unique idea." [21] This simplicity is perfect
beauty, and appears as if a divine solar disk
were traced within the "square" of human
genius.

The measure of Apollo opposed to the super-
exuberance of Dionysos. The sublimely-beauti-
ful in him wrestles with boundless monstrosity.
"He exceeded the limits of human nature; his
genius, tending to soar beyond time and space,
seems to exhaust itself in vacuum. However
great his measure, he exceeded it," writes Ségur
on the campaign of 1812. [22]

It is this touch of the immeasurable in his
schemes, like the titanic building of the Atlantes, which strikes terror into poor Decrès'
heart: "The Emperor has gone stark mad! Mark
my words; some day he will send us all to the
devil, and it will all end in a terrible catastrophe." [23] Or, in Napoleon's own words: "the
impossible is merely a bogey for the timid and
a refuge for cowards." [24] Here, indeed, that
which is boundless borders on madness; here
the tri-dimensional geometry but paves the way

[21] Antommarchi, I.
[22] Ségur, V.
[23] Marmont, III.
[24] Houssaye, *1815,* III.

to that of the fourth; the square of human genius becomes the base of a divine pyramid narrowing to a single apex, one point where man exclaims: "I am God."

Yet even this boundless titanic super-exuberance is through a medium of a different order—sacrifice, finally subdued by him to a sense of divine measure.

His will-power too, like his mind, presents a like combination of contrasts, another instance of the square of genius.

Peace and War, Worker and Leader, such are the two "discordant-concordant" aspects of his will-power. In war, instantaneous lightning—hyphen-like flashes; in peace, methodical effort, the drop wearing out a stone.

It is hard to determine which of his two sayings is most expressive of his will: The soldier's: "One must stake all for all"; [25] or the worker's: "I should like a rest, but the ox is yoked and must draw the plough." [26] It is hard to determine when the hero in him appears most sublime: in the triumph of victory, or in the humility of toil; when swooping like one of the eagles on his colours into the din and

[25] Bourrienne, II. "Il faut jouer le tout pour le tout."
[26] "J'aimerais plus de repos; mais le boeuf est attelé, il faut qu'il laboure."

clamour of battle, or plodding like a patient ox in peaceful toil.

"Work is my element, I am created for it. I can gauge the limit of endurance of my feet, or of my eyes, but that of my work I have yet to find." [27] "I am always at work: at dinner, in the theatre; if I wake in the night, I begin to work. To-day I woke at two, and sat on the sofa by the fire to look through the war-office reports sent in last night, in which I discovered twenty mistakes and this morning returned them to the Minister of War, who is now busy rectifying them." [28]

Three times a month he received from the Ministry of Finance voluminous in octavo reports with long columns of figures, which he verified so minutely that a mistake of a few centimes did not escape him. Every fortnight or three weeks he looked through the reports of the Ministry of War, compiled in separate rubrics: service lists, division, corps, artillery, infantry, engineering and conscript muster-rolls, reports on foreign armies and so on, and so on. [29] He reads them with avidity: "I find more pleasure in an army report than a young

[27] *Memorial,* III.
[28] Roederer.
[29] Fain.

lady in a novel." [30] Sometimes he says admiringly: "this report is so well written, it reads like a beautiful poem!" [31]

And all this knowledge was stored in his mind systematically, like honey in the cells of the honeycomb, or more prosaically, for he prefers prose, like "files in the drawers of an office bureau." "When I have done with one subject, I close the corresponding drawer, and open another, so that my various jobs never overlap one another, and there is neither confusion nor fatigue. And when I feel sleepy I shut up all the drawers and fall asleep at once." [32]

Men are weak, because they are absent-minded. Genius is all attention, and attention is the mind's will-power. Napoleon possessed that mind-will in the highest degree. "Force and continuity of concentration are characteristic features of Bonaparte's mind," writes Roederer, a member of the Council of State. "He can work eighteen hours at a stretch on the same or on different subjects, and however physically tired he might be, or under however severe a strain, or angry, I never saw his atten-

[30] Lacour-Gayet.
[31] Lévy.
[32] *Memorial,* III.

tion flag or lose its flexibility, neither would he be diverted from the task immediately in hand. No man was more absorbed in the work of the moment." [33] "The capacity of his mind which allows him to transfer at will and concentrate his attention and all his powers at a moment's notice on what is most important, is marvellous, no matter if it is a midget or an elephant, a single man or a whole army. Anything outside the task he is bent upon simply ceases to exist: It is a kind of sport, from which nothing can divert him." [34]

Men may tire; not so gods, nor the eternal forces of nature; so was he, too, indefatigable.

"His collaborators were exhausted and crushed beneath the burden he imposed on them and which he carried himself without apparently feeling its weight." [35] "As First Consul he used to preside at the departmental meetings of the Ministry of the Interior from ten o'clock in the evening to five in the morning." "Often at St. Cloud he would keep the members of the Council of State from ten o'clock in the morning till five in the afternoon with a quarter of an hour's break, and appeared to be as fresh at the

[33] Roederer.
[34] Pradt, *Histoire de l'Ambassade de Varsovie en 1812*. Taine.
[35] Taine.

end of the sitting as at the beginning." [36] "I was able to discuss any topic for eight hours on end, and pass on to another with my mind as fresh as ever. Even now (at St. Helena) I could dictate for twelve hours at a stretch." [37] "He works fifteen hours without either food or rest." [38] "In one of these sittings, during the Consulate, the Minister of War fell asleep; other members nearly dropped from their seats from fatigue. "Wake up, citizens, wake up!" exclaimed Bonaparte, "It's only two o'clock. We must earn the salaries we receive from the nation." [39]

During the seventy-two days of that last campaign in France, people wondered when he found time to eat or sleep.

After the terrible Leipzig *débâcle* he left Mainz on the 2nd November, 1813, and late next day, on the 3rd, descended from his carriage in the courtyard of the Tuileries: he made the journey from Mainz to Paris without a single halt. "When he left the carriage his legs were so swollen that he could scarcely stand, and his face was livid from fatigue. Nevertheless, after hastily embracing wife and son, he spent the rest of the day with his minis-

[36] Pelet de Lozère. *Opinions de Napoléon au Conseil d'État.*
[37] Gourgaud, II.
[38] O'Meara, I.
[39] Roederer.

ters, hearing their reports, dictating and issuing orders. He dismissed them at six in the morning, commanding the Minister of Finance to return at mid-day. "You will bring the reports on the exchequer, we must look through them together." Napoleon's secretary, Baron Fain, told Count Lavalette that in those days "the Emperor went to bed at eleven, rose at three in the morning and worked till late at night without a minute's respite. "This must be stopped, or it will be all over both with himself and me."[40]

"He accomplished more in these three years (of Consulship) than kings during a century," says Roederer.[41] "My achievements are boundless, but what I sought to accomplish was greater still," is his own verdict.[42]

And this state of superhuman, seething, inconceivable energy lasted without truce or respite for thirty years.

"Such men are not made of flesh but bronze," says Dostoievsky's Raskolnikov of Napoleon. Nay, they are of flesh, and very weak flesh too, weaker perhaps than that of ordinary people.

The First Consul looks so fragile, that "one

[40] Lévy.
[41] Taine.
[42] *Memorial,* III.

doubts if he can live a week." [43] Grown stronger in after years, he nevertheless catches cold in the slightest draught; cannot sleep in the light; vomits at the smallest overdose of food; cannot endure tight boots or the smell of fresh paint; like a woman is easily moved to tears or fits of faintness. His nerves are generally over-sensitive. "My nerves are in such a state, that I would go mad were it not for my exceptionally slow blood circulation." [44]

In him the spirit triumphs over the weakness of the flesh. "I always had complete control over my body." [45] According to the Apostle Paul there is a "natural" and a "spiritual" body; the "psychical" and the "pneumatic." Napoleon is one of the world's greatest *"pneumaticians,"* though not of course in our Christian sense. In him the pneumatic body almost visibly reveals itself through the wrappings of the natural body. It seems as if there lay the beginning of Napoleon's "magic."

In the gloomy chambers of the Tuileries he leads the stern life of an ascetic. Abstinence and sobriety are inborn in him. He eats little: "However little I eat—it is always too much." [46]

[43] Vandal, *Bonaparte,* II.
[44] Rémusat, I.
[45] Antommarchi.   [46] Fain.

He drinks only water mixed with red wine. Hurries through his meals; eight minutes for lunch, fifteen for dinner; sometimes forgets to dine. Makes love to women with equal haste. "Women held sway over him for perhaps five or six days in the year, and even then . . ." Josephine remarks sadly. The only luxuries he indulged in seemed to be snuff, liquorice with aniseed to refresh the mouth, eau de cologne and hot baths.

Utterly disinterested: though the wealthiest sovereign in Europe, he himself never owned any property; even Malmaison was purchased in Josephine's name. "Each one to his taste," he would say: "I was fond of building but not of property." [47] He left France almost penniless; when, on St. Helena he was obliged to sell his silver plate, and was interred at the expense of his gaolers—the British.

Flesh is immobility, spirit is movement. He was all spirit, all movement, as if a lightning were imprisoned in a human body.

"One might think that he wants to realize the *'perpetuum mobile,'* wrote the British commissioner from Elba: "He likes to tire out the companions of his walks. While afoot he seems

[47] Fain.

incapable of sitting down were it only to write. After walking about in the scorching heat from five in the morning till three in the afternoon, and visiting the frigates and transports, he went for a three hours' ride, 'for a rest,' as he told me himself." [48]

In 1809, during the Spanish war, he covered the thirty-five Spanish leagues between Valladolid and Burgos in five hours; starting with a numerous retinue, he left them behind one by one and galloped into Burgos almost alone. [49]

When out hunting he covered hundreds of miles. At Castiglione, in the first Italian campaign, he ran down five horses in three days.

Walking, he is equally tireless. Paces five or six hours up and down the room unheeding. [50] Is fond of talking as he walks: "It seems as if he could go on like this all day long."

His inner impetus corresponds to the outward. "Clouds driven across the sky by a gale move less rapidly than do his emotions and thoughts." [51] "That is why he never can write: his hand cannot keep pace with his mind. He dictates. and that so rapidly as if he were talk-

[48] Houssaye.
[49] *Memorial,* I. Ségur, III. Fain.
[50] Fain.
[51] Bourrienne.

ing to his correspondent; anyone listening at the door would think he was listening to a dialogue." "He never repeated a sentence twice and could never stand being interrupted." This incapacity to repeat his thought was due to its absolutely organic, living quality. "He even dictated as it were on the move; the rapidity of his thought could be gauged by that of his steps." [52]

It seems as if no man on earth had ever been in motion more than he. And for such a man— St. Helena, "the punishment of quietude"; the devil himself could not have invented for him a more terrible hell.

"My achievements are boundless, but what I sought to accomplish was greater still." Who says that, Napoleon the lord of the world? No, the builder of drain pipes. . . . "One has to accomplish as much as I have, to realize how difficult it is to benefit people. . . . I spent nearly thirty millions on drain pipes, and yet no one will so much as thank me for it." [53]

The sun of Austerlitz is visible to all, but the drain pipes are not: neither those underground, nor those political ones which drained off the bloody trough of the Revolution. Yet where

[52] Fain.
[53] *Memorial,* III.

does the countenance of the hero wear a more godlike aspect—when lit up by the sun of Austerlitz, or in the darkness surrounding drain pipes?

Here is yet another aspect of Napoelon "the unknown" and humble. Like the Assyrian sun-god, the gigantic winged-bull, he has harnessed himself to the plough, and tirelessly draws it through the furrow: "I should like a rest, but the ox is yoked and must draw the plough."

The precision of his work is perhaps even more marvellous than its immeasurable volume. Such precision and conscientiousness belong not to men but to gods or to the eternal forces of nature: only the stars rise in the heavens or gods render unto men with such miraculous mathematical precision.

With childish glee he points out a mistake of twenty centimes in a report dealing with millions of francs. One day, meeting one of the ladies-in-waiting with the Empress's laundry bill in her hands, he took it from her and declared the laundry charges too high; began to bargain over each item and compelled the prices to be reduced.

Cutting the gilded tassel off the magnificent new upholstery in the Tuileries palace he put it in his pocket; a few days later he produced it to the major duomo with the remark: "God forbid I should suspect your honesty, *mon ami,* but you are being swindled: you paid for this one third more than its actual worth." [54]

The Demiurge, the god-Worker, is the same whether ruling suns or atoms. "Thou hast been faithful in a few things, I will make thee ruler over many things." Had he not haggled over twenty centimes the miracle would not have happened—that almost instantaneous, in the course of three or four years of consulship—transformation of France, the beggar maid, into the opulent queen of the world.

Three weeks before the end, in the interval between two fits of vomiting "stuff black as coffee residue" from the cancerous ulcer of the stomach, he sits up in bed and holding in his lap a file of papers, dips his quill in an inkstand, held in front of him by his chamberlain, and writes a codicil to his will under schedule A, in which he includes items omitted before: "all my quilts and mattresses, half a dozen shirts, half a dozen handkerchiefs, cravats, towels, socks, a pair of sleeping trousers, two dressing gowns, one pair of suspenders, two

[54] Lacour-Gayet.

pairs of hose, and a small box filled with my snuff." [55] He bequeaths all these to his son.

"How *bourgeois!* At such a time he should be thinking of his soul!" thus from our "Christian" point of view; not so for him, who is a "pagan." For his whole soul is condensed in one great love of the Earth: whether in his dream of world-dominion, or in the solicitude for a pinch of snuff—it is the same love.

"I bore the world on my shoulders" (*"J'ai porté le monde sur mes épaules"*). If our senile Europe still holds out, is it not because this Atlas, this titanic apocalyptic *bourgeois* is still bearing her weight upon his shoulders. . . .

[55] *Memorial,* IV.

CHAPTER VII

THE LEADER

THE face of Napoleon the Leader appears in its true aspect only when one realizes that War with him was not supreme. As a "super-real being" he knows too well the historical inevitableness of war in his time; knows that war is still mankind's "natural state." Yet here, as everywhere, he passes through what to men seems "natural" to that which to them appears as "supernatural"—through the necessity of war to the miracle of peace. For his chief aim—world domination, the universal unity of the nations—signifies the end of all wars and the advent of everlasting peace.

"In order to do justice to Napoleon, all the great deeds which he was not allowed to accomplish should be weighed in the balance." [1] He was allowed to accomplish great deeds only in war, but never in peace. Yes, though it may seem strange, Napoleon is a peacemaker. Always at war, but longing for peace; he more

[1] *Memorial,* I.

than hates, he despises war, at any rate in his highest moments. Has he not understood and all his life remembered the howling of that dog over the body of its master lying on the field of battle; understood or felt that this humble creature in its love was above him, the hero, in his hatred—war.

"What is war? A barbaric trade." [2] "War will become an anachronism. . . . The future belongs to peace: a time will come when victories will be won without guns or bayonets." [3] Such sentiments might easily fall from the lips of such an ideologue of peace as Leo Tolstoy; coming from Napoleon, they acquire a stupendous and terrible significance. The will for peace and the will for war—thus in him are these contradictions profoundly united, forming, as yet perhaps unknown to him, the most profound "square" of genius.

"A general is the most intelligent among the brave"; [4] thus he defines the genius of the Leader. To complete his idea one should say: "a commander is the bravest of the brave and the wisest of the wise." [5] Men absolutely brave are rare; absolutely wise—rarer still. Of those

[2] Lacour-Gayet.
[3] J. Bertaut.
[4] Bertaut.
[5] J. Bertaut.

who unite both these qualities there are none, or one may appear once in a thousand years. Napoleon feels himself to be such a man: "thousands of years will pass before a man like myself appears again."

"The science of war consists first of all in considering well every opportunity, and then making a precise, almost mathematical calculation, of how much must be left to chance. . . . But this ratio between knowledge and chance can only be properly estimated by the mind of a genius."

"To mediocre intellects chance always remains a mystery and becomes a reality only to the outstanding."

The secret of chance, the mystery of destiny is Napoleon's secret *par excellence,* because he is "the Man of Destiny."

"Eternity, Æon—is a child playing at dice," said Heraclitus. Chance, fate, the "star" are the dice of Eternity. War too is the "game of chance" of the Leader with Destiny. "To stake all for all" is the rule of the game. No one ever played it with such mathematical precision, such a geometrically clear perception and with such prophetic vision as Napoleon.[6] "My great

[6] Gourgaud, II.

talent is to *see clearly* . . . this is the straight line
which is shorter than the curve." The joining
of chance to mathematics, of that which is the
most blind with that which is clearest vision,
such is the intellectual "square" of military
genius.

Before the beginning of each campaign or
before every big battle he would spend days
on the floor poring over a huge outspread map
studded with pins with wax multi-coloured
heads to mark the actual or supposed position
of his own and the enemy's troops; planning the
marvellous order with which units would be
transferred across hundreds and thousands of
miles—from the camp in Boulogne on the
shores of the English Channel to the banks of
the Rhine, or from the mountains of the Sierra
Morena into the Russian steppes; converging
marches, incessant offensives, lightning blows—
the whole strategic plan is as simple and beautiful as a work of art or a geometrical theorem.
The main object is so to place the adversary before the opening of hostilities, as to render impossible for him all communication with his
base. Marengo, Ulm, Iena, Austerlitz—were
all different adaptations if this method. Here
everything is mathematics and mechanics: "the

force of an army, similar to the volume of movement in mechanics, is measured by the mass multiplied by rapidity; the rapidity of the marches increases the courage of the troops and the chance of victory." [7]

Infinite caution, a seeming "cowardice" on the part of the leader, is here better than courage. "None is more cowardly than myself when drawing up a plan of campaign I exaggerate every danger . . . and experience the most poignant anxiety, which, however, does not prevent my appearing to be perfectly calm to those around. I am then like a woman in childbirth (*comme une fille qui accouche*). But no sooner I arrive at decision than I forget everything except that which may bring me success." [8]

To forget everything at the last moment is as difficult as it is to remember everything to the last moment. Slow mechanics, a geometrically clear perception—at first, then—sudden clairvoyant vision, and prophetic lightning.

"Woe to the leader who brings a ready-made system to the field of battle." [9] Suddenly to get rid of system, knowledge, wisdom, to shed them

[7] Bertaut.
[8] Roederer. This was said almost on the eve of the 18th Brumaire.
[9] Bertaut.

like a useless burden, is even harder than to be laden with them.

"War is a strange art: I have fought sixty big battles and learnt nothing beyond what I knew already at the first." [10] "I always had the inner consciousness of what awaited me." The "inner consciousness," or primary knowledge prior to experience is that very "magnetic premonition," spoken of by Bourrienne; the innate "knowledge as a remembrance," the *anamnesis* of Plato. It does seem as if, within the space of thousands of years, no man had been gifted with it in such a degree as Napoleon.

"It seemed as if Mack's (the Austrian field-marshal) plan of campaign had been drawn up by myself." "Mack's Caudian Gorge will be Ulm," prophesied Napoleon, and as he had foretold, so it happened: at the exact day and hour foreseen by him Ulm was surrounded.[11] The plan of Austerlitz was carried out with similar precision: the sun of victory shot out its first rays at the very day, hour and moment when commanded to by Napoleon. On the morning of the battle of Friedland, before he was victorious, he calmly ate his breakfast with the bullets whizzing around, and his face

[10] Gourgaud, II.
[11] Lacour-Gayet.

187

was radiant with a joy, which spoke more clearly than words that already he knew—"remembered" that victory was his. Yes, indeed, he *remembers the future* as if it were the past.

"The great art of battle consists in altering one's operation lines during action; that is my idea, quite a novel one." [12] This is only possible if the plan itself is organic, absolutely non-mechanical; it remains in the mind of the leader flexible to the last like molten iron in a furnace.

"During the greatest battles absolute silence reigned around Napoleon; had it not been for the more or less distant roar of the guns, one could have heard the buzzing of a wasp; people dared not even cough." [13] Amid this silence he listened to the inner voice of his "demon-counsellor," according to Socrates, to his "magnetic premonition."

The moment at last is at hand when he must "stake all for all."—"The fate of battles is determined by one minute, one thought—a moral spark!" [14] "A battle is always a serious affair, but victory sometimes depends on a trivial matter—a hare." [15] This "hare" is the humble mask worn by destiny—"eternity playing at dice like

[12] Gourgaud, II.
[13] Stendhal.
[14] *Memorial,* I.
[15] Gourgaud, II.

a child." The battle of Borodino was lost because Napoleon had a cold, that of Waterloo because the rain did not cease in time.

It is at this last moment that comes that lightning flash of will by which the Leader settles everything. "Nothing is so difficult and at the same time so important as to know when to make a decision." [16]

"Very seldom did he meet in men the moral courage of two o'clock in the morning." "I mean unprepared courage which is necessary on an unexpected occasion and which in spite of the most unforeseen events leads to freedom of judgment and decision." "He did not hesitate to declare that he was himself eminently gifted with this two o'clock in the morning courage and that in this respect he had met with but few persons who were at all equal to him." [17]

"I believe I am the bravest man in war who ever existed," he says simply without a shadow of boastfulness just because the conversation turned that way. [18]

With him military bravery is by no means the main feature. It is but a fraction of that

[16] *Memorial*, I.
[17] *Ibid.*
[18] *Memorial*, IV.

"after midnight" courage of which he spoke so well. "After midnight" courage in a dual sense, direct and metaphorical, as yet perhaps incomprehensible even to him: the noon of will, of action over, the midnight of sacrifice and suffering will set in; but in both hemispheres the sun of courage will remain one and the same.

One had to be blind not to see that Napoleon was brave in war. Tolstoy and Taine were thus blind. The measure of their blindness gives the measure of their hatred. Taine even tries to prove that Napoleon was a coward. And many "conscientious" judges believed it and rejoiced. "He is a coward, like ourselves!"

It is difficult to say when Napoleon was bravest of all. It seems that from Toulon to Waterloo and onwards to St. Helena, to his last breath —he was always the same. "He lived in a state of continuous enlightenment," says Goethe. But to France the first vision of the young hero's image, of a beauty not seen by man since the days of the Epaminondes and Leonidas, was revealed in his deed at Arcola.

Towards November, 1795, the position of General Bonaparte, Commander-in-Chief of the army in Italy, became almost desperate. His small army was dwindling away in unequal combats: twenty thousand exhausted men were pitted against sixty thousand fresh troops. No help from France was forthcoming. The flower of the army—officers and men were casualties. The hospitals were crowded with the wounded and sick, a prey to the malignant fever of the Mantuan marshes. Napoleon himself was ill. But worst of all, the morale of the army was low after the unsuccessful attack on the height of Caldiero where the Austrian Field-Marshal Alvinzi had fortified himself on an impregnable position and menaced Verona, and from where Bonaparte for the first time in his life had been compelled almost shamefully to retreat.

He wrote in those days: "Citizen Directors, maybe we are on the eve of losing Italy. I have done my duty, so has the army. My conscience is clear, but my soul is torn asunder. . . . Help, send us help!" He knew that none would be sent: the Jacobins, the Royalists, even the Directors themselves were only waiting for the opportunity to get rid of him. "There is no more hope," he wrote to Josephine, "everything is lost. . . . Only courage is left to me." [19]

"Any other general but Bonaparte would

[19] Ségur.

have retreated beyond Mincio, and Italy would have been lost," says Stendhal who took part in the campaign.[20]

But Bonaparte did not retreat. He thought of an insanely daring manœuvre. To march to the rear of the Austrians from the almost impassable marshes of the Adige and taking the enemy by surprise to force him to battle on three narrow dykes where numerical superiority was of no advantage and the issue depended on the valour of the troops. In order to carry out this manœuvre, it was necessary to seize at a single and sudden stroke a small wooden bridge across the marshy river Alpena at the end of one of the dykes near the village of Arcola—which was the sole means of communication connecting the rear of the Austrian army across the marshes.

At dead of night and in complete silence the French army left Verona. The troops were so elated by Bonaparte's bold manœuvre that the wounded joined the ranks straight from their cots. Creeping in the dark across the dykes of the Adige, the advanced columns of the French under the command of General Augereau approached the Arcola bridge before daylight.

[20] Stendhal.

The Leader

Contrary to Bonaparte's expectations the bridge was well defended: two battalions of Croats supported by artillery were able to keep it under a terrific flank bombardment, but it was too late to retreat, besides there being nowhere to go: there was equal destruction in front as in the rear; they were caught in a trap.

The first column advanced to attack, and was entirely wiped out by a volley of grape-shot, like rubbish swept off with a good broom. So were the second, third and fourth columns. The men ran on to the bridge only to be at once swept off by the broom. They perished aimlessly. All of them—smooth-cheeked lads, the *sans culottes* of '93, also in their own way "Plutarch's men." But even such hot-heads were loath to die needlessly: it was as impossible to capture the bridge as it was to jump up to the sky. Nearly all the commanders were either killed or wounded and the men refused to advance into the firing line. When Augereau rushed forward with the colours and thinking he could rally the soldiers to follow him, shouted in a rage: "Why are you so frightened of death, you scoundrels!" no one followed him.[21]

[21] Lacroix.

Napoleon

Bonaparte galloped up and saw at once that if the bridge were not taken all was lost; that not he would take Alvinzi by surprise but the reverse. On hearing the din of battle, Alvinzi would crash down from the heights of Caldiero, rout the whole French army and drown it in the marshes. In a flash Bonaparte realized what he had to do. He jumped off his horse and seized the grenadier's colour. The men did not or dared not understand what he was going to do; they halted gazing at him in silence. There he stood in his plain short dark-blue tunic with scarcely any embroidery, a wide silk scarf round his waist, in white buckskins and low goatskin turn-over boots; thin and slight as a sixteen-year-old girl in spite of his twenty-seven years; his long scarcely powdered hair hanging limply over his sunken cheeks; a look of strange calmness as of deep thought on his face—only a fierce gleam like that of molten metal in his great eyes. The face of a sick boy, which had specially endeared him to the soldiers and for which they "pitied" him.

Still they did not realize what he was going to do. In one arm he raised the colour—the sacred tattered emblem pierced by bullets, in the other his sword; turned round, shouted:

"Soldiers, are you no longer the victors of Lodi?"—and ran on to the bridge.[22]

They all rushed after him with one thought: better to die themselves than see "the sick boy" killed. The officers surrounded him, shielding him with their bodies. General Lannes, twice wounded, shielded him from the first volley and fell wounded a third time. Colonel Muiron covered Bonaparte from the second volley and was killed on his breast, the blood spurting on his face.

A hailstorm of grape-shot mowed the men, but still they advanced and reached the end of the bridge. Only here they could not stand the almost point blank firing, turned and ran back. The Croats pursued them finishing off with bayonets those who had escaped the grape-shot.

Bonaparte still remained standing on the bridge. A group of grenadiers caught him by the arms and dragged him away out of the firing line, but in the scrimmage let go of their hold, and failed to miss him. He fell in the bog and sank up to the waist in the mire, struggled only to sink still further. It was good to stand as a hero on the bridge but disgusting thus to wallow in the marsh like a frog. He heard, so one thought,

[22] Ségur.

even through the din of battle nothing but the gentle rustling of the dry rushes around his head; saw nothing but the quiet grey sky above, and himself quieted down, awaiting the end: perchance to be sucked in by the quagmire, perchance to be killed or taken prisoner by the Austrians; or maybe, he knew—"remembered"—that he would be saved.

The Austrians were already about forty paces ahead of him, but as yet had either not seen or failed to recognise him, with his face smeared with the blood of Muiron and covered with mud. And so the quiet sky watched over him. . . . There, on the bridge, death was imminent; here in the bog he was safe; the deeper he sank, the better he was protected from the flying bullets. The grenadiers recovered their senses only when they reached the bank; they saw that Bonaparte was missing. "Where is he? Where is Bonaparte?" they yelled in horror. "Run back, save him, save him!" They ran back on to the bridge, overthrew the Croats by a frantic onslaught, caught sight of Bonaparte in the bog, now sunk almost to the arm-pits, managed to reach out to him, pulled him up, brought him to the shore and placed him on his horse. He was saved.

The Leader

What happened afterwards it is difficult to understand, just as every battle, which in its essence is chaos, is difficult to understand. Those who take part in it are often unable to give a comprehensive account of it. One thing is certain: Bonaparte's manœuvre had failed. The bridge was not taken either on that day, or the next; only on the third day General Massena crossed it almost without fighting, because it had been abandoned by the Austrians. The centre of action had then shifted into another zone.

Was Bonaparte's exploit, therefore, useless? No; it was useful in the highest degree. "I assure you all this was absolutely necessary to obtain a victory," he wrote to Carnot, though not of his own exploit, which he seemed to have forgotten about, but of Lannes.[23] Yes, all this was necessary to raise the spirit of the soldiers, to ignite that "moral spark which decided the issue of battles." The will-discharge from the soul of the leader produced countless corresponding counter flashes in the soul of the soldiers. It was as if a spark had fallen into a powder magazine, and it exploded.

Such miracles happened in the three days

[23] Ségur.

that followed after Arcola that the brave,
clever and firm Alvinzi became almost frantic
in trying to realize what was taking place and
why Bonaparte's troops suddenly appeared to
have gone mad. Having once lost his self-control, Alvinzi began to make blunders: abandoned the impregnable Caldiero position, sur-
rendered Verona, Mantua, the whole of Italy.
This was what Bonaparte won by sitting in a
bog. Arcola, the Pyramids, Marengo, Austerlitz, Iena, Friedland are pearls strung on the
same necklace; had its thread then snapped at
Arcola, the whole necklace would have been
broken.

A few minutes before his death in his delirium he spoke of a battle on a bridge, perhaps
of this very *"pont d'Arcole."* [24] At that moment
he was about to cross another and more formidable bridge. Did he cross it or did he again fall
into the bog? Even if he did—no matter: he
will be saved, as he was then.

"The enemy was defeated at Arcola. . . . I
am rather tired," he wrote to Josephine just as
in his letter to Carnot making no mention of his

[24] Antommarchi, II. The dying Napoleon uttered distinctly only
two words: *"tête-armée."* Probably *"tête"* meant *"tête de pont"*—
bridge head. The meaning of the delirium: "bridge-army," the
"battle of the Bridge."

exploit.[25] In general, he never could vaunt of
his courage before people, were it only because
his courage was quite different from what
people call by that name. If man knew before-
hand all that would happen to him up to his
last hour, neither our human fears nor our
human courage would exist for him. But
even so Napoleon knew—"remembered"—the
future. Not always, oh no, only at rare moments, also very terrible ones, but of a different, inhuman kind of terror, and to overcome
which he needed a different superhuman courage.

It was in moments such as these that he felt
himself to be miraculously immune in the midst
of battle. He had fought sixty big battles and
countless small ones, nineteen horses had been
killed from under him.[26] and yet he had only
been wounded twice: rather severely at the
siege of Toulon in 1793, and lightly at Ratls-
bonne in 1809.

Every battle is, as it were, a gamble between
man and death, a toss-up of "heads or tails."
The chances to win diminish in geometrical
proportion to the increase of stakes; but in a
case of continuous winning the similitude be-

[25] Masson, *Mme. Bonaparte.*
[26] O'Meara, II.

tween what we call "chance" and that which
we term a "miracle" grows in equal progres-
sion. Napoleon's invulnerability in battle appears in the nature of such a miracle.

> Clad in mighty armour no danger thou reckest:
> An invisible guardian is given thee, warrior.

Only if possessed by that feeling of immunity
could he play with death as he did. Marshal
Berthier who stood beside him on the firing line
at Essling endured it for a long time but exclaimed at last: "If Your Majesty will not go
away from here, I will order the grenadiers to
drag you away by force!" [27]

At the battle of Arsis the Emperor himself
placed the guards in battle array on a plot of
ground where shells were bursting continu-
ously. When one fell just in front of the column,
the men instinctively recoiled; they rallied immediately, but Napoleon wanted to give them
a lesson. He spurred his horse and compelled it
to approach and stand over the smoking shell.
It exploded, the horse—its stomach torn open,
dropped dead dragging down the rider. He
disappeared in a cloud of dust and smoke, but
picking himself up at once, mounted a fresh

[27] Constant, II.

horse and galloped off to continue the forma-
tion of the next battalions.[28]

Courage is as contagious as cowardice. Courage is ignited from courage as one candle from
another. But in order to set a whole army
aflame, like dry timber in a forest fire, from a
ingle "moral spark," the "lightning flash"
ch decides the fate of the battle, the timber
be dried and the men seasoned. It is ex-
what Napoleon does do: by slow, hard
k he raises the soldiers' receptivity to the
us of courage; he trains the men how to die.
To train them well, it is necessary to live
eir life, to be one with them. And he does
ive the soldiers' life; it is easy for him to do
so. That which is simple and childlike in his
nature draws him towards the simple folk:
"thou hast hid these things from the wise
. . . and hast revealed them unto babes." "The
wise men," the "ideologues" hate Napoleon, the
simple folk love him. To them he is the greatest among men and yet also the "Little Corporal," they worship the great man and pity the
"little one." "I talked and jested with the
simple soldiers in the camp. I always felt proud
of having sprung from the people." [29]

[28] Houssaye, 1814.
[29] O'Meara, II.

When on the island of Elba he would spend six hours at the barracks, inspecting the bedding, tasting the soup, bread and wine, chatting to the men as their equal: and being as was his custom "stern to the superiors and kind to the subordinates." [30]

On the most bitter and humiliating day his life, the 7th of June, 1815, when he dicated his power—that is himself—bef paltry Chamber, he forgets everything to of soldiers' boots. He writes to Mar Davout, Minister of War: "I saw with conc that the troops dispatched this morning h only one pair of boots each, whereas there a plenty in stock. The men must be given tw pairs to carry in their knapsacks and a third to wear." [31] He knew or pretended to know every soldier, before each parade he learnt by heart special lists with the names of the men.

Only here, in Napoleon's army was revolutionary equality perhaps fully realized. "The whiskered old grenadiers would never dare address the youngest subaltern as they do the Emperor." [32]

In Egypt, beneath the scorching sun of the

[30] Houssaye, *1815,* I.
[31] Houssaye, II.
[32] Lévy.

desert among the ruins of Pelousia the soldiers gave up to him the only narrow strip of shade under a crumbling wall; he realizes that this is "no mean concession."[33] He repays his debt to them later in the Syrian desert when he orders that all the horses—including his own—should be given over for the use of the sick and wounded. A heathen, he remembers the Christian commandment: "A general must treat men as he would wish to be treated himself." [34]

Perhaps there is here even something more than revolutionary equality—it is almost a religious confraternity.

At one of the halts on the march from Elba, nearing Grenoble he drinks wine out of the same pail and the same tumbler as all his "whiskered grenadiers." "Together they taste wine and blood out of the common cup."

When the Emperor, wounded in the leg at Ratisbonne, his wound scarcely dressed, jumps again on his horse and rushes into the fray, the men weep with emotion. "Blood is soul," the ancients knew this well, and the simple folk know it still. With blood spilt "the soul of the leader passes into the souls of the men." [35] The

[33] Lévy.
[34] O'Meara, I.
[35] *Memorial,* III.

whole army—from the last soldier to the marshal—are one soul in one body.

It is easy to understand why the soldiers
served no one so loyally as they did Napoleon.
"With the last drop of blood gushing from their
veins, they cried: *"Vive l'Empereur!"* It is easy
to understand why those two grenadiers at Acre
shielded him with their bodies from the frag-
ments of an exploded shell; why General
Lannes, twice wounded, again threw himself
into the *mélée* at Arcola and was wounded a
third time, and why Colonel Muiron was killed
on Bonaparte's breast. It is easy to understand
why General Vandamme was ready to "pass
through a needle's eye and rush into the fire"
for the Emperor, and General Gopoule when
Napoleon embraced him before the ranks at
Landsberg exclaimed: "to be worthy of such an
honour, I must die for your Majesty!" and was
killed next day in the battle of Eylau.[36] And
Colonel Soure at Jemappes who while his arm
was being amputated dictated a letter to the
Emperor refusing his promotion to the rank
of General. "The supreme grace which you
could vouchsafe me would be to let me remain
a Colonel in my regiment of the Uhlans whom

[36] Marbot, II.

I hope to lead to victory. I refuse the rank of
General. May the great Napoleon forgive me!
The rank of Colonel is the most precious to
me." No sooner was the surgical bandage applied to his bleeding stump of an arm, than he
mounted his horse and galloped back to his
regiment.[37] One can understand why Count
Ségur overcame pain and the fear of death
during a surgical operation by the mere thought
of his leader: "how good it is to die, to be
worthy of him!" [38] And what of the old veteran
of Marengo sitting at the roadside at Waterloo, his legs smashed into pulp and repeating
in a loud and firm voice: "It's all right, boys,
forward march, and *vive l'Empereur!*"

But the most miraculous revelation of such
contagious courage seems to have been at
Essling.

News is suddenly brought that the bridges
across the Danube connecting the French army
with its operation base on the island of Lobau
are destroyed and the reserves under the command of Marshal Davout cut off. The position
of the army stretched across a wide plain, deprived of its base, its reserves and supplies becomes so desperate that at the war council

[37] Houssaye, *1815,* II.
[38] Ségur, III.

the marshals in a body voted for the surrender
of Lobau and a retreat to the right bank of the
Danube. The Emperor hears them patiently,
but decides not to retreat. "That is right, that
is right! That is the way to do it!" exclaims
Marshal Massena, a general of the Revolution,
the grandson of a tanner and son of a soap-
boiler, former smuggler and shopkeeper, an in-
corrigible thief and extortioner, who robs his
own soldiers; withal the saviour of France, the
victor over Suvorov and "the beloved son
Victory." "That is the way to do it, yes!"
repeats enthusiastically, and the dim eyes
this puny little man are ablaze with a wondrou
light. "Ah, here is a great heart, here is a genius
worthy to command over us!" Here Napoleon
takes him by the arm, leads him aside and whispers caressingly in his ear: "Massena! you must
defend the island and finish what you have so
gloriously begun. You alone can do it. You will
do it." Yes, he will. The soul of Napoleon has
entered Massena's soul; the brave has caught
fire from the brave, like one candle from another.

A few hours later, when the position becomes
still more desperate, and the last terrible dis-
patch that Marshal Lannes is fatally wounded

is received, Napoleon's self-control gives way. For the first time in his life he weeps in the midst of a battle, as if his courage had forsaken him; but rallying immediately he dispatches General Montion with a message to Massena that he must hold out at Aspern, the chief approach to Lobau, "if only for four hours longer." Seizing Montion's hand and gripping it with such force that the imprints of his fingers long remained visible, Massena replies: "Tell the Emperor that no power on earth will compel me to leave this place, I will stay here four hours, twenty-four hours—forever!" And he stayed. So heroic was the defence of Aspern that the enemy only dared enter its ruins on the next day after the French rearguard had abandoned the village.[39]

"Without me he is nothing, with me—my right hand," says Napoleon of Murat,[40] and could have equally said so of all his marshals: they all were but members of the Leader.

Yes, the whole army was one body and one soul. "He is a wizard," Murad-Bey's Mamelukes said of Napoleon: "he has bound his soldiers together with a big white rope and when he pulls it hither and thither, they all move to-

[39] Ségur, III. Marbot, III.
[40] O'Meara, II.

gether as one man." [41] This "white rope" is "magic"—the lightning-will of the Leader.

"However great was my material power, my spiritual one was greater still: it bordered on magic." "Sire, you always work miracles!" was the unsophisticated but profound testimony of the deputy-mayor of Macon.

Ségur wrote in his reminiscences: "Whenever he (Napoleon) wished to seduce, his manner was one of irresistible charm, a kind of magnetic force." [42] The person he wishes to attract seems to become "beside itself." In those moments of sublime power he no longer commands like a man but seduces like a woman. Herein lay the significance of "his *embonpoint* which did not belong to our sex," of his strange likeness to "a young female beauty," which he saw in himself, or to an "old governess" of the Empress Marie-Louise which misled the old provincial footman. This was one of his "wizard tricks" which had so frightened the superstitious Austrian: "damn that changeling, now he's turned himself into a woman!"

The god Dionysos too is a "changeling." In the bacchantes of Euripides he is "like unto a woman"—"thelymorphos," while in the Licurgus of Aeschylus he becomes a real Androgenes. In the Eleusinian mysteries Dionysos-Bacchus is called "diphyes," there being in him two natures, the male and female. What does it mean? It means that the divine plenitude of human personality, the "square of genius," is to be found in the union of its two severed halves—sexes—the two contrasts; the perpendicular of the square is represented by masculinity, activity; the base, by femininity, the spirit of sacrifice. Or, according to Kant: *"Erst Mann and Weib zusammen machen den Menschen aus,"* ("Only Man and Woman united make up a human being"). The divine spark of human personality is set alight only by the joining of the two poles, feminine cathodes and the masculine anodes.

Napoleon was nearer to Alexander the Great, his fore-image than he thought. Alexander's ambition was to be "a second Dionysos." "Dionysos" means "son of god": *"Dio"*—"god," *"nysos"*—"son." That is why an old disabled soldier of Napoleon's army, whom Léon Blois knew in his childhood, "was unable to distinguish the Emperor from the Son of God." That is why Napoleon's soldiers as in the Dionysian mysteries, drank with him of the same cup of wine and blood and became one body and one soul, which was the Great Army.

When in 1805 the Emperor by a motion of the hand throws the Army from the camp at Boulogne on the shores of the English channel to the banks of the Rhine, its movements are so rapid, so marvellously ordained, that anyone watching them from above might take them to be the rhythmic dance of a Dionysos chorus with the god himself as leader.

> And it seemed like a god, from on high
> He soared, watching o'er all, above them;
> With the light of his wondrous eyes,
> The moving spirit of all.[43]

Those eyes with "the intolerable blaze as of molten metal" were the eyes of Dionysos himself.

"I want my colours to inspire religious fervour." [44] But what religion is this?

"Whose voice is this? Who calls us? *Evoe!*" Thus do the bacchantes of Euripides recognise their invisible god. The same voice speaks in Napoleon when he says: "as I rode past the ranks in the fire of battle and cried: 'soldiers, unfurl your colours, the hour has struck!'—you

[43] Tyutcheff. Translated by Miss Margot R. Adamson.
[44] Lacour-Gayet.

should have seen our Frenchmen: the men *danced* with joy; hundreds of men became as one, and with such as they everything seemed possible." [45]

The men danced like madmen as if possessed by the god, like bacchantes. "Napoleon's soldiers are like men possessed," says a witness on the eve of the battle of Waterloo.[46] This "frenzy"—*katakhe,* in the mysteries of Dionysos was a sign of "the presence of the god."

Those whom Napoleon wishes to seduce seem to become beside themselves. This state of "being beside oneself," of ecstasy, *ekstasia,* is also a sign of divine presence. To enter into god, man must come out of himself. He must come out of this human, unreal, fractional, mortal *"ego"* in order to enter into the divine, real, entire and immortal. This is the meaning of "He that loveth his life shall lose it, and he that hateth his life . . . shall keep it."

Dionysos is a teacher of ecstasy; so is Napoleon. Dionysos, the son of Semela—a mortal woman—is a man who becomes god; so is Napoleon. Dionysos is a conqueror and peacemaker; Napoleon too wants to unite West and East and found a world power—the kingdom of ever-

[45] Lacour-Gayet.
[46] Houssaye, *1815,* II.

lasting peace. Dionysos is the suffering man-god; and Napoleon on St. Helena, a Prometheus chained to the rock, is that same Dionysos.

"The eyes of the universe are fixed on us. Even here we are the martyrs of an immortal cause. We here struggle against the oppression of the gods and the prayers of the nations are for us," says he, as Prometheus himself might have said.[47]

Perhaps it is here at St. Helena that his courage is most sublime, not any longer a sudden flash, but a continuous "two o'clock in the morning" courage. "I have certainly committed errors in the course of my life, but Arcola, Rivoli, the Pyramids, Marengo, Austerlitz, Iena, Friedland—are *rocks* of granite: the tooth of envy is powerless against them."[48] No, even these are not granite, but mist, phantoms, beyond which rises the everlasting granite of St. Helena, the Holy Rock, *Pietra Santa*—everlasting courage.

"Who says he's grown old? Why damn him, he has strength for sixty more battles in his body!" exclaimed an old British soldier on catching sight of the Emperor at St. Helena.[49]

[47] *Memorial,* I.
[48] Lacour-Gayet.
[49] *Memorial.*

He himself said in 1817: "I am not yet fifty, my health is fairly good; I have at least thirty more years to live."[50] "It was said that I had turned grey after Moscow and Leipzig, but as you see, even now I have no grey hairs, and I hope I am able to bear greater reverses than these." [51] "You disbelieve me, but I do not regret my past grandeur; you see me slightly affected by what I have lost." [52] "It seems as if nature itself created me to endure great misfortunes; my soul beneath their blows was like marble; the lightning did not smash it, but merely grazed it." [53] "Adversity was wanting to my career. Had I died on the throne enveloped in the dense atmosphere of my power, I should to many have remained an enigma but now misfortune will enable all to judge of me without disguise." [54] His nudity—Napoleon without disguise—means St. Helena, the Holy Rock, immutable courage. "I stand on a rock." (*"Je suis établi sur un roc,"*) says he at the summit of his glory, and might well say the same in the depth of his fall.[55] Who of all men was raised to such heights or fell as he? The deeper the fall, the higher his courage. All his glories may

---

[50] Gourgaud, II.
[51] *Memorial*, I.
[52] *Memorial*, III.
[53] *Memorial*, IV.
[54] *Memorial*, I.
[55] Roederer.

be dimmed except this: *the master of courage.*[56]

He is ever true to himself in this. Whether in generously sacrificing his life at Arcola, or in stingily haggling over twenty centimes in the report of the Minister of Finance, or in remembering the pinch of snuff left in the snuff-box which he bequeathed to his son. . . . All these are the manifestations of the *same frenzied ecstatic courage.* Napoleon is the teacher of ecstasy and courage because these two forces are inseparable. To attain that ultimate courage which overcomes the fear of death man must shed the mortal and enter the immortal *ego.* "The greatest enjoyment of oneself comes in moments of danger," says Napoleon,[57] then one rejoices in and is drunk with that most intoxicating wine of Dionysos—one's own divine *"ego,"* which is immortal in the face of death.

> All, all that destructively threatens
> For the heart of the mortal holds hidden
> Ineffable rapture . . .
> Perchance immortality's token . . .[58]

[56] Maurice Barrès, *Les Déracinés.* Barrès, rather unsuccessfully calls Napoleon "a professor of energy, *le professeur de l'energie.*" Least of all Napoleon resembles a "professor"; the word "energy" is too abstract to be applied to such an organic phenomenon as Napoleon's courage. But the idea is correct.

[57] Bertaut.

[58] Pushkin. *The Feast in a Plague-stricken City.* Translated by Miss Margot R. Adamson.

The Leader

This is why the second name of Dionysos is *Lyseus*—the Liberator: he liberates the souls of men from that most terrible thraldom, the fear of death.

In this, however, as in all else Dionysos is but the shadow of Him Who Cometh: "whosoever believeth in Me shall never see death."

Men are grateful to those who teach them how to live; but maybe they are still more grateful to those who teach them how to die. That is why Napoleon's soldiers are so grateful to him, that with the last drop of blood gushing from their veins they shout: *"Vive l'Empereur!"* He is, in truth, the Leader of human souls, teaching them to vanquish the last enemy —Death.

"One must want to live and know how to die," says Napoleon.[59] And also: "A soldier must know how to die."[60] To vanquish the last enemy—death, every man must be a soldier on the field of battle. Is it impossible? "The impossible is merely a bogey for the timid, a refuge for cowards," is Napoleon's answer. Every man, in order to die and to rise again must be a Napoleon.

All of us, who are demoralized by pseudo-

[59] Ségur, II.
[60] Thiébault, IV.

"Christianity" more or less believe like poor
Nietzsche that to be good signifies being weak,
and to be strong means being wicked. Napoleon
knows that this is not so: "goodness is strength,
a strong man is good, only the weak are evil." [61]
He says this at the beginning of his life, he repeats it at its close. "Be good and brave always," is his last bequest to his Old Guard on
bidding them farewell at Fontainebleau after his
abdication. He might have bequeathed this
message to all mankind.[62]

"I have shown what France was capable of;
let her live up to it." [63] He has shown what men
are capable of; so let them too live up to it.

The sources of ecstasy—that wine of Dionysos—are now tarrying within our hearts, just
as the waters of a well tarry during a drought.

"Christian" mankind is ruled by "dry"
Americanism. "I am the true vine, and My
Father is the gardener." We have forgotten this
and no longer drink of the fruits of any vine.
It is true, that we are "dry" only of wine, but
not of blood. We have only just drowned the
world in blood, and we are "drying" now, perhaps only to become "soaked" once again.

[61] Masson, *Manuscrits.*
[62] Bourrienne, V.
[63] J. Bérault.

The Leader

Napoleon also shed blood, but he was never "dry" as we are. He was the last to taste of Dionysos's vine; the last intoxicated intoxicator.

Dionysos is merely a shadow; the substance is the Son of Man. Is not the substance better than the shadow? Yea, better; but when the substance disappears, only the shadow remains. The world cannot live without the Son, and if not by His substance, it lives by His shadow. The shadow of the Son is Napoleon—Dionysos.

The first shadow within human memory of the same substance of the Son is the ancient Babylonian hero Gilgamish; of him the nomad tribes of Senaar sung perhaps a thousand years before the day of Abraham. Gilgamish, the Sun-hero, wandering over the face of the earth in search of the Plant of Life, follows the way of the sun from East to West; and sinks like the Sun into the ocean whither "Atlantis" too had sunk,[64] and there he finds the Plant of Life.

"That Plant is like unto the Rose and the Thorn." [65] The Thorn of Suffering, the Rose of Love. Such is the wisdom of Dionysos: by way

[64] D. Mérezhkovsky, *Les Mystères d'Orient: Egypte, Babylone,* ed. de l'Artisan du Livre, Paris, 1927. D. Mérezhkovsky, *The Mystery of the Three* (in Russ.) by "Plamia," Prague, 1925, on the relation of Gilgamish to Atlantis.

[65] Gilgamish.

of the lacerating Thorn of Death—to the intoxicating Rose of Immortality.

Napoleon too follows the path of the sun from the day hemisphere into that of night. The last man from Atlantis, the last Sun-hero, like the Sun, he too sinks into the ocean and there finds the Plant of Life—the torturing Thorn and the intoxicating Rose of Dionysos.

The first Dionysos is Gilgamish, the last—Napoleon. And what has been said of the first, may well be applied to the last:

He saw all around, to the bounds of creation,
He drank of life's cup to the dregs.
His gaze penetrated the depths of all mysteries,
The secrets of wisdom were fathomed by him . . .
A message he brought us from ages primordial.
He wandered afar, in travail and sorrows,
The story of which he inscribed on these tablets . . .
Two-thirds he is god, and one-third mortal man . . .[66]

[66] Gilgamish, I.

Chapter VIII

COMMEDIANTE

THE clouds flew so low over the mountain peaks of St. Helena, that they appeared as if clothed in the trailing garments of ghosts. "One of Napoleon's favourite pastimes was to watch the clouds as they rolled over the highest point of that gigantic mountain, and as the mists wreathed themselves into fantastic draperies around its summit, sometimes obscuring the valleys from sight, and occasionally stretching themselves out far to sea, his imagination would wing and indulge itself in shaping out the future from those vapoury nothings." [1]

Nay, not the future but the past; already he knows that he has no future. St. Helena is a tomb in which he is buried alive. And these swiftly flying clouds in their fantastic forms and ghostly shapes are but visions of his past, the dreams of by-gone days. "What a ballad (*roman*) my life has been!" says he to his fel-

[1] Abell, Mrs. L.

low captives on St. Helena. "What a ballad,"—
a dream, a phantom, a flying cloud.

"I sometimes imagine I am dead, and only
a kind of vague consciousness remains that I am
no longer there," the Empress Josephine kept
repeating before her death.[2] Napoleon on St.
Helena could have said the same.

"Provided this would last!" *"Pourvou que cela
doure!"* Napoleon's mother would murmur like
a clairvoyante Parca, in her broken French; an
unassuming, retiring old lady, "the mother of
kings—the mother of sorrows," as she called
herself.[3] Nay, it did not last, drifted away like
vapour. "Letizia was always firmly persuaded
that the entire vast edifice (the empire) would
collapse." [4] "No dream could equal what she
lived through." *"On ne rêve pas comme elle a
vécu."* These words spoken of her might well
be applied to her son.

"As a result of so many years of convulsions,
sacrifice and bloodshed France has obtained
nothing but glory," declared Alexander I, the
Emperor of Russia, to Napoleon's marshals assembled in Paris in 1814 after its occupation by

---

[2] "Il me semble quelquefois que je suis morte et qu'il ne me
reste qu'une sorte de faculté vague de sentir que je ne suis plus."
[3] "Je suis la mère de toutes les douleurs."
[4] Stendhal.

the Allies.[5] "Nothing but glory"—vacuity, phantasms, flying clouds. . . .

Is that so? Have all his deeds faded like a dream? No, some of them remain: there remains the judiciary backbone inserted into Europe's body with the Napoleonic Code, that chart of the individual rights of man laid down for the first time since Roman days, by universal legislature. And if modern Europe is able to withstand the onslaught of Communistic depersonalizing influence, it will perhaps be due to the fact that Napoleon's backbone is still strong within her.

A grandson no longer remembers nor knows his grandsire, though recalls his features in his own countenance; thus to modern Europe Napoleon is "unknown," though she still wears a Napoleonic profile. Is this little or much? A great deal when compared to the achievements of others; very little, compared to what he wished to do and might have accomplished,—so little indeed, that he deemed it to be "almost nothing." He himself foresaw how history would belittle him: "I will be almost nothing." *"Je ne serai presque rien."*

Yes, though "a super-real being" he was ever

[5] MacDonald, *Souvenirs*, ed. 1910.

vaguely conscious that the seeming reality of things was all illusion, and that he created his life as the sleeper his dreams, the artist images, the musician symphonies.

He strives for power over the world merely to shape the world according to his dream. "I love power as an artist, or as a fiddler loves his fiddle. I love it for the sake of drawing from it sounds, melodies and harmonies."

"The world as a representation. *Die Welt, als Vorstellung.*" Perhaps he would realize the meaning of this, when the vapour-curtain rose over the rocks of St. Helena. *"Vorstellung"*— the tragedy of Dionysos with the world as a stage, with himself as poet, actor and hero all in one: he writes, acts and perishes in it.

If he is a "monster," it is one of a different nature and stature than Nero; yet it seems he too, like that other, might have exclaimed when dying: *"Qualis artifex pereo!"* "How great an artist perishes in me!"

Like the god-Demiurge he creates a dream-world; when the dream fades—the god dies.

> Farewell my beauteous dreams,
> I leave you unfulfilled,
> Lo, like a god, I die,
> Amid beginnings of creation.[6]

[6] Maikov, *Three Deaths.*

Commediante

"Commediante!" Pope Pius VII, the captive of Fountainebleau, and victim of "the new Nero and anti-Christ" is alleged to have exclaimed, in the course of the dispute over the second Concordat of 1813. This apparently is a legend. Yet even if apocryphal, this definition is most profound. A "comedian" indeed, in a humanly-divine comedy.

When Napoleon was planning the ceremonial of his coronation, the artist Isabey and the architect Fontanes brought him a miniature model of the interior of the Cathedral of Notre Dame, in which it was to take place, and a number of dressed-up puppets all numbered. Napoleon was delighted with this toy. He at once summoned Josephine, his ministers, courtiers and marshals, to a rehearsal of the "puppet-show"—the sacred rite of coronation.

On the retreat from Moscow when he learnt of the half-witted General Malet's conspiracy for the overthrow of the dynasty, he exclaimed: "So my dynasty is no firmer than this! One man, a runaway lunatic, is sufficient to shake it! It means that my crown is hardly secure on my head if a plot hatched in my very capital by three adventurers can shake it."[7] Yes, the

[7] Lacour-Gayet; Masson, *Napoléon et son Fils*. Masson, *Joséphine répudiée*.

crown on his head is but the tinsel crown of a
puppet emperor, and his power is no more sub-
stantial than a dream.

Yet barely a few months since as he stands
on the summit of the Poklonnaia hill gazing at
Moscow lying at his feet, he is braced, after
calamities past and before terrible calamities
to come, by the sight of this wonderful pano-
rama unrolled before him like the setting of
some phantasmagoric play. "The applause of
the nation seemed to greet us." [8] From ancient
Thebes to Moscow, such are the expanses of
time and space encompassed by this vast
dream.

Then instantly everything disperses, fades
away like a mirage or a passing cloud wafted
away as by a gentle breath, by the news: "Moscow is empty." [9] Empty as an empty dream.
And the setting changes too: "Moscow disappears like a phantom in volumes of rolling
flames and smoke." [10] "It was the most magnificent and awful *spectacle* I ever beheld," he
recalls it on St. Helena.[11] And there among the
charred ruins of Moscow, he sets up a French
theatre—a spectacle within a spectacle—a

[8] Ségur, V.
[9] *Ibid.*

[10] Ségur, V.
[11] O'Meara, I.

dream.[12] This already is the second degree of the "world as a representation" (*Welt als Vorstellung*) ; no longer a number but a logarithm.

"General Bonaparte saw an *imaginary* Spain, an *imaginary* Poland (Russia) and now sees an *imaginary* St. Helena," says Hudson Lowe.[13] And this means, that from beginning to end, his will to live was the will to dream.

> "We're of such stuff as dreams are made of,
> And our little life is rounded with a sleep."

These words of Prospero—Shakespeare—he would interpret thus: to build one's dreams out of the stuff the world was made of, and one's own world out of the tissue of dreams.

"The most realistic of beings"—and the most idealistic—two aspects of him, and who shall say, which of them is the real one?

The same in great things as in small. "He was fond of everything which inclined towards reverie: the poems of Ossian, subdued light, melancholy music. He loved to listen to the murmur of the wind, spoke with rapture of the roar of the sea; was inclined to believe in ghosts and was generally superstitious. Sometimes, in the evenings, coming into Mme. Bona-

[12] Gourgaud, I.
[13] Ségur, V.

parte's salon, he ordered all the candles to be shaded with white gauze; we had all to remain silent while he told us ghost stories . . . or, listening to subdued and slow music, he would fall into a kind of trance which none of us dared interrupt by the slightest movement." [14]

The subdued spectral light, these shaded candles seemed to be a forecast of that sunlight breaking through the vapour-phantoms hovering over St. Helena.

One night he acts an improvised romantic story of two unhappy lovers, Terese and Guilio, in which there also figures a mysterious being, an Androgyne-Sybilla, recalling sometimes Napoleon himself and sometimes Dionysos the Changeling. [15]

"Guilio stabbed Teresa's heart with a dagger," and with these closing words he approached the Empress making as if he were drawing a dagger from its sheath. The gesture was so realistic, that the ladies-in-waiting

[14] Rémusat, I.

[15] Bourrienne, III. Guilio, conte improvisé, par Napoleon. "On vit paraitre a Rome un être mysterieux qui prétendait devoiler les secrets de l'avenir et qui s'enveloppait d'ombres si épaisses que son sèxe même était l'objet de doute et de discussion. Les uns . . . decrivaient les formes et les trâits d'une femme, tandis que les autres justifiaient leur effroi en lui donnant l'aspect d'un monstre hideux." Napoleon himself is "the Corsican monster"; he too possesses "magnetic clairvoyance," and "un embonpoint qui n'est pas de notre sèxe." (*Memorial*, II.)

shrieked and threw themselves between him
and Josephine. Feigning not to notice the impression produced, Bonaparte like a consummate actor, continued his narrative. "Carried
away by his imagination, he would utterly forget his surroundings." It was rumoured that he
had lessons from Thalma the celebrated actor,
"though perhaps he himself might have taught
him a few things." [16]

"When dictating his army orders, he resembles an Italian improviser or Pythia on her
tripod." [17] So here, on the fields of battle, he is
also the comedian, improvising as in Madame
Bonaparte's salon "a ghost story," the title of
which is universal history; and the smoke-bil-
lows of battle writhe and roll like the vapours
from the Pythian crevice, or the phantom
clouds over St. Helena.

A magician, calling forth visions, or in our
modern phraseology a producer of giant films,
grand master of striking artistic contrasts.

General Bonaparte, Commander-in-Chief of
the army in Egypt, grants a safe-conduct to the
monks of Mount Sinai "out of reverence to
Moses and the people of Israel whose cos-
mogony is reminiscent of by-gone ages," and

16 Bourrienne, III.
17 Bourrienne, IV.

writes his name in the "golden visitor's book next to that of Abraham." [18] Is this too, "acting," "quackery," flashlight propaganda in the clouds, or an apocalyptic sign? Yes, all these perhaps, and more. Perhaps he is sincerely convinced of his exodus out of time into eternity, out of universal history—into cosmogonic eschatology.

Here are different masks out of the same "commedia." He rhapsodises of how he and the Empress will spend his old age "in visiting, with my own horses like a plain country couple, every corner of the empire; in receiving complaints, redressing wrongs, in doing good everywhere and by every means! . . . These were among my dreams! . . ." [19] Here, it is the lion in sheep's clothing: he knows perfectly well this will never be, though, perhaps, he sincerely cherished the illusion of this *bourgeois* idyll; for the *bourgeois* in him was stronger than it appeared.

To commemorate his famous words uttered on the battlefield of Eylau: "Awful spectacle! A sight such as this should inspire rulers with a love of peace and abhorrence of war," he orders the painter Gras to paint a picture of

[18] Bourrienne.
[19] *Memorial*, III.

himself standing on the field among the slain,
his eyes full of tears, raised to heaven.[20] 'Twere
better not to have ordered it, to have ceased for
once playing the "commediante"; yet this by
no means signifies that he did not sincerely
abhor war.

Meeting a convoy of Austrian wounded, he
orders his retinue to halt, and doffs his hat with
the exclamation: "honour and glory to these
unfortunate heroes!"[21] A theatrical gesture
Thalma himself might have envied, though
again this does not necessarily exclude its sincerity.

He consoles a poor young Russian lad, Count
Apraksin, taken prisoner at Austerlitz and sob-
bing like a child, with the empty words: "Calm
yourself, young man, and know that there is no
shame in being beaten by the French."[22] Better
to have abstained from such consolation;
though L. Tolstoy's exaggerated indignation
over this "piece of acting" was perhaps due
to his own whilom participation in another and
subtler kind of "acting" at so-called "truthful-
ness."

He knows that Josephine is barren. Out of

[20] Rémusat, III.
[21] Ségur, II.
[22] *Ibid.*

pity and loath to divorce her, he proposes that she should feign a *grossesse* so that he might proclaim his son by another woman as his heir. Josephine consents, and the plan fell through only on account of Corvisart's (the court physician) flat refusal to take part in the fraud. Taken all together, it is a most singular combination: touching compassion for his ageing wife, childlike helplessness in resorting to a fraud strange to find in such a realist as he; the dream to found a dynasty on a spectre, a foundling heir,—the whole scheme is the limit of "farce," "quackery," which it is impossible either to justify or even to explain, unless one accepts the theory that if the world is a dream, a "presentation," and everything in it is unreal and a delusion, one extra fraud does not matter especially if engineered for a good purpose?

Josephine complains that "in all their long years together Bonaparte had never for a moment been sincere." [23] Is that so? He may have been perfectly sincere according to his own lights, but then sincerity and truth, as he understood them, were different from hers. "Bonaparte is so funny!" *"Il est drôle, Bonaparte!"* she had exclaimed after their first meeting. Only

[23] Constant, I.

such a twittering canary from Martinique, as was Josephine, could fail to realize that he was not "funny" but "terrible." Mme. de Rémusat felt this and wept from fright, like a child.[24]

"Comedian," "actor," yet no hypocrite; ever acting a part, not another's but his own: Napoleon acting the part of Napoleon. In this sense he was truth itself, but a truth so fantastic that no one believed it. "My secret inclinations, which come from nature, provide me with endless opportunities for deception." It is these same "natural inclinations" which make of him a being of another sphere of creation, a man belonging to a different cosmic cycle—æon, not of 1800 A.D. but 1800 B.C., or of some equally far-off future age; a man from "Atlantis" or of the "Apocalypse." To deceive all around him, he had but to remain perfectly true to himself. As a matter of fact, he has no desire to deceive, —he merely conceals his true self so as not to terrify men by the "miraculous-monstrous" in him; for this he wears a mask, puts a veil on his face when he descends to the people out of the cloud of Sinai.

Himself deceiving none—he is deceived by all. It seems as if no monarch ever was deceived

[24] Rémusat, I.

and betrayed to such an extent as he—by ministers, marshals, wives, mistresses, brothers, sisters, enemies and friends. However strange it may seem, but he was by nature artless and simple; if anything, too straightforward, and frank to cynicism, as in the assassination of the Duc d'Enghien or in the "dirty trick" with the King of Spain. First he naïvely surrenders himself to Alexander I, "that wily Byzantine," then to the Emperor of Austria, his father-in-law, and finally to the English. When he came to his senses he was already at St. Helena: "My romantic and chivalresque opinion of you (the English) has cost me dear." [25]

"These people refuse to parley with me," he complains to Caulaincourt in 1814 during the Congress of Chalons. "Times have changed. . . . They have forgotten how I treated them at Tilsit. . . . My magnanimity amounted to foolishness. . . . A mere schoolboy would have shown more cunning than myself. . . ." [26] Perhaps his ruin was brought about by too much honesty. He is absolutely devoid of the capacity "to change the front," *"changer de manœuvre"*; [27] or of the flexibility of the spinal cord, an art

---

[25] O'Meara, I.
[26] Thibaudeau (Fouché).
[27] Lévy.

in which Talleyrand and Fouché, these verte-brae-less vermin, excel. "Courage cannot be faked: it is a virtue devoid of hypocrisy." [28] And it is his virtue *par excellence; "Pietra-Santa,"* "the Holy Rock"—a rigid backbone.

"We are able to understand one another," the Emperor of Russia, Paul I, writes to Bona-parte the Consul.[29] They can understand one another because both are "romantics," "knight-errants" and strange to say, Don Quixotes.

"Napoleon was supremely conscious of mili-tary honour, the brotherhood of arms. . . . This wily politician was always a *chevalier sans re-proche* (a knight without reproach)," says Vandal, one of the few of Napoleon's conscien-tious judges.[30]

How unlike he is to Taine's *"condottiere,"* to *Il Principe* of Macchiavelli—a "cross-bred be-tween the lion and the fox!" No, here it is a cross-bred of the lion and the dragon: the might of a lion on the wings of a dream.

To him everything is a phantasm; yet this does not signify that everything is but "the pall of Maya" over an absolute void. Napoleon, like Goethe, is an absolute antithesis of the Buddhist

[28] J. Bertaut.
[29] *Memorial,* IV.
[30] Vandal, *Napoléon et Alexandre I.*

233

doctrine of the will towards absolute non-being and impersonality. They both are the eternal *yea* as opposed to the eternal *nay*.

> Alles Vergängliche
> Ist nur ein Gleichnis.
> (All that is transient
> Is but a symbol.)

Goethe but expresses what Napoleon experiences: things temporal are but a symbol of things eternal. The sleeper dreams of what befell him in his waking hours, and he, who lives within time—of that which was and will be in eternity. "The world as a 'presentation' fades away; there remains 'the world as will-power.' This will-power is denied by Buddha and Schopenhauer, and affirmed by Napoleon and Goethe.

Mists, dreams, phantoms—and beneath them —St. Helena, the Holy Rock, *Pietra-Santa*— everlasting granite. His visible day-name is Courage; his secret, night-name—Destiny.

CHAPTER IX

DESTINY

"ALL my life long I sacrificed everything—rest, happiness, fortune, to my destiny."[1] This is Napoleon's face unmasked—the absolute truth of him, absolute sincerity. When he says: "destiny," he hands us the key to that closed door which guards his secret. But that key is too heavy for us to wield: the door remains closed, and Napoleon "unknown."

What is destiny? Chance, which rules the world, *"le hasard qui gouverne le monde,"* as he sometimes thought himself.[2] Chance is a blind devil, and Napoleon, the lord of the world, is but its slave. Or is it a superior force endowed with vision and at one with the hero's own will? Perhaps, he himself never even gave it a thought; though it seems as if his thoughts ever hovered *round it,* and plunged into those depths wherein was buried the solution of Destiny's enigma to mankind. Himself, he never looked the Sphinx straight in the face,

[1] Masson, *Le Sacré de Napoléon.*
[2] *Memorial,* IV.

yet the consciousness of the Sphinx gazing into *his* own face never left him; and this also he knew, that if he failed to solve the enigma, the monster would turn on and devour him. The face of Œdipus as he gazed at the Sphinx was full of thought, so is Napoleon's. The peculiar feature of his face, which strikes one as setting it apart from all other human faces, is its infinite brooding thoughtfulness. The longer one gazes at it, the deeper grows the impression that he is brooding not only over himself, but over our common destiny, that of the entire "Christian" mankind, which in its great recantation spurned the meek yoke and bowed to the iron yoke of Fate.

The night before the battle of Iena, the Emperor walked alone to the outposts to inspect a roadway which was being blasted in the Landgrafen cliffs for the artillery. It was a dark night, nothing was visible ten paces ahead. As he approached the line of sentinels, one of them, hearing the sound of footsteps, shouted: "Who goes there?" and took aim. So deeply was Napoleon engrossed in his thoughts that he did not hear the challenge and walked on. The sentinel fired. The bullet whizzed past the Emperor's ears. He fell flat on the ground, and it was well he did so: the sentinels all along the line opened fire, and a swarm of bullets passed over his head. After this first volley, he got up, approached the nearest post and disclosed his identity.[3]

The lord of the world falls to the ground as if to worship some other Lord greater than himself. Who is it he worships? The dark demon—chance, or that radiant "star" of his, the nocturnal sun—Destiny? His thoughts a while ago, though not of this, may yet have hovered round it, just a hairbreadth away, as he himself had had a hairbreadth escape from death.

A few days before his abdication and attempt at suicide in Fontainebleau, he was in such a profound state of reverie, that "when persons entered the apartment in answer to his summons, he failed to notice them; looked at them as if unseeing, and sometimes more than half an hour would elapse before he addressed them; as if recovering from a trance, he would question them and appeared scarcely to heed their answer." There was no means to rouse him from this kind of lethargic reverie, *"préoccupation pour ainsi dire léthargique."* [4]

[3] Constant, II.
[4] Constant, IV.

Napoleon

In 1810 a gala reception was held at Compiègne after the celebration of the marriage with Marie-Louise, to which were bidden the first dignitaries of the empire, the ministers, marshals, foreign ambassadors, ruling princes, kings and archdukes. Napoleon left the *salle de jeux* and entered the drawing-room. The whole crowd of courtiers pressed after him. "When he reached the centre of the apartment," writes an eye-witness, General Thiébault, "the Emperor stood still, crossed his arms on his breast, fixed his eyes on a spot about six paces in front of him, and remained thus motionless as if turned to stone. Everyone stood still too in a wide semi-circle round the room with bated breath in complete silence, at first scarcely daring to look at each other; then began to exchange glances as if asking the meaning of this strange scene." Five, six, seven, eight minutes elapsed. The bewilderment grew; no one could make out what had happened. At last, Marshal Marmont, who stood in the front rank of the courtiers, approached him softly and whispered something so low that no one heard. "No sooner, however, had he done so, than the Emperor, without moving and his eyes still fixed on the ground, replied in a thundering voice:

Destiny

"What business is it of yours?" *"De quoi vous mêlez-vous?"* And the marshal, a patriarch of military glory, "the beloved son of Victory" and the conqueror of Suvorov, backed to his place abashed and discomfited. Napoleon still remained motionless. "At last, as one *rousing himself from sleep,"* he raised his head, uncrossed his arms; his searching glance swept the assembly, turned silently and went back to the *salle de jeux*. In passing by the Empress, he threw her a curt "Come!" and together they withdrew to their private apartments.

"All this I recall as if it were but yesterday, —but fail to understand its meaning," concludes Thiébault. To him the scene appears as an undignified farce, *"jonglerie."* "I had never felt so insulted in my life before; never had the despot in Napoleon stood out so shamelessly and arrogantly revealed." [5]

Thiébault, poor fellow, feels his insult so deeply that he forgets a different impression produced on him by Napoleon: "There is nothing I can compare to the feelings experienced in the presence of this titanic being." Had he but recalled them, he might perhaps have realized that in this scene at Compiègne Napoleon

[5] Thiébault, IV.

was neither a "juggler" nor a "despot." Where
then was the "insult"? On Napoleon's part in
any case it was purely involuntary; he had not
the slightest desire to insult anyone if only for
the reason that he saw no one; at such times
people for him ceased to exist, they faded away
like shadows. Herein, apparently, lay the
nature of the insult.

Thiébault's bewilderment is ours also. What,
indeed, did this "lethargic reverie," so akin to
lethargic sleep, signify? He sees, hears, acts, is
more wide-awake than anyone—but all this outwardly; inwardly he is asleep, an everlasting
dreamer, a somnambulist of his nocturnal sun
—Destiny; he walks, as it were, along the very
brink of the chasm; if he wakes, he falls; but
waken he shall not, until the last step into the
abyss.

He sleeps, and his heart-beats are as faint as
those of a lethargic sleeper. "I think my heart
does not beat; I never feel it." [6] "I seem to have
no heart." [7]

Waking—he sleeps; and sleeping is awake.
Dreams are interwoven with reality, dreams en-
croach into reality, not only in a metaphysical
inner sense, but also physically and outwardly.

[6] O'Meara, I.
[7] Gourgaud.

Destiny

On his way to the Opera the 24th December, 1800, he falls asleep in the carriage and dreams that he is drowning in the Italian river Tagliamento; he is roused on the brink of death by the explosion of the infernal machine.

He sleeps on the fields of battle, "during the combat,—far in the rear of the firing line." [8] This even becomes a habit: "I am accustomed to sleep during a battle." [9] Like a child in its cradle he slumbers, lulled by the roar of the cannon. At the most decisive moment, when his fate hangs in the balance, suddenly he falls asleep, as if disappearing somewhere in quest of the unknown.

Before the battle of Austerlitz, he was so sound asleep "that they could scarcely wake him." At Wagram, at the climax of the battle, suddenly he orders a bearskin to be spread on the ground, lays himself down and drops into dead sleep; this lasts about twenty minutes; on waking up he continues to give orders as if he had never been asleep at all. [10] During the disastrous evacuation of Leipzig, when the whole front is crumbling, he remains calmly asleep in

[8] *Memorial*, II.
[9] Ségur, II.
[10] Ségur, III.

a chair for two hours; he was only roused by the explosion of the bridge across the Elster by which the retreat was cut off, and the army destroyed.

As in war—so in peace. He is fond of working, getting out of bed between two sleeps. It seems as if Napoleon's genius, clairvoyance, is but that narrow isthmus of vigilance between two gulfs of dreams.

"What to think of Napoleon's dreaming which lasts from Vendemiaire to Waterloo?" asks Léon Bloy: "He awoke only to find himself before the face of God." Neither the greatest calamities, not even his fall could finally wake him. "He is still asleep at St. Helena." [11] And in his sleep he dies, or wakes into death.

"He asked me what kind of death I thought was the easiest; and added that being frozen to death was considered the best, because one died sleeping . . . *si muore dormendo.*" [12] Dr. O'Meara recorded his conversation with Napoleon at St. Helena.

Even so he died in his sleep, frozen to death by the icy breath of Destiny.

[11] Léon Bloy.
[12] O'Meara, I.

Destiny

Storms and the sea rocked our bark;
I slept, to the waves' chance abandoned:
And two of them, seizing upon me,
Played with me, tossed me at will.
All around us the rocks rung like cymbals,
Winds whistled, the wild billows sang.
Stunned, tossed I in sounding Chaos:
O'er the sounding Chaos hovered my dream.

A dream on the seas—on "the many waters."
"The waters which thou sawest . . . are peoples
and multitudes and nations and tongues," says
the Angel of the Apocalypse. The many waters
of the West is the Atlantic, wherein was en-
gulfed Atlantis, and had set the suns of the first
human race and that of the last man from Atlantis—Napoleon.

O'er the sounding Chaos hovered my dream,
Vivid as fever, bewitchingly silent.
O'er thunderous darkness lightly it flitted,
In delirious lightnings it kindled its world,
Green was the earth, shining the æther. . . .

Æther radiates a light more brilliant than our
own; the earth is verdant with the freshness of
the dawn of a primordial world. . . .

"Mansions and gardens, labyrinths, columns. . ."

The titanesque building of the ancient
Atlantes . . .

Napoleon

"Methought I heard rustling numberless crowds;
Many I recognised, faces unknown. . . ."

Faces belonging to a different human race . . .

"Enchanted creatures I saw, magical birds. . . ."

Creatures of another world . . .

"Proudly I paced the heights of creation,
Motionless below me, glittered the world. . . .
In the thick of dreams like a sorcerer's savage yelling
Sounded the thundering roar of the deep. . . ." [13]

The substance of Atlantis is magic and so is
that of Napoleon: he himself conjures up the
visions of his dreams. It is the dream of all mankind, the beginning and end of universal history: Atlantis and the Apocalypse.

That is why he, a great magician and a
sorcerer, himself creates his own dream.

And into the peaceful realm of visions and dreams
Rushed, foaming, the roaring billows. . . .

Wars, conquests, the rise and fall—all these,
like lightsome dashes of spray, break into a
dream.

His dream is prophetic. "He possessed a kind
of magnetic premonition of his future destinies,"
"une sorte de prévision magnétique de ses futures

[13] Tyutchev, *A Dream at Sea*. Translated by Miss Margot R. Adamson.

destinées." [14] "I always had an inner sense of what awaited me." [15] Men are blind to the future, he was not: he knows, *remembers* it, as if it were the past. "Sight is the mean between touch and foreboding," thus with that mathematical precision which is inherent to him he defines these vague presentiments. The hand says to the eye: how can you see two miles off when I cannot touch that which is two paces away? The eye says to presentiment: how can you see the future, when I cannot see two miles away? [16]

In the happiest moments of his life after Marengo he says: "Nothing ever happened to me which I did not foresee, and I alone did not wonder at what I had accomplished. I also foresee the future and will attain my goal." [17] If that goal was world dominion—then he failed to reach it. The way is clear, the goal—darkness; he knows what and how to do, but knows not the wherefore. "I feel as if I am being driven towards an unknown goal." (*"Je ne sens poussé vers un but que je ne connais pas."*) [18] How could he fail to believe in his *predestination,* when

[14] Bourrienne, IV.
[15] *Memorial,* IV.
[16] Gourgaud, II.
[17] Miot de Melito, *Mémoires,* ed. 1880, I.
[18] Ségur, IV.

events which at first seemed to go against him and remove him from the objective he had in view, finally turned to his advantage. Was not he like a man, who was being led by some irresistible power, as a blind man is led by the hand whither he knows not? [19] Blind—but clairvoyant:

The Fated Executor of a Command *Unknown.*

At dawn, on the day of Waterloo, "when on the banks of the Sambre, the Emperor approached a bivouac fire, accompanied only by his aide-de-camp on duty (General C . . .). Some potatoes were boiling on the fire, and the Emperor asked for one, and began to eat it. Then, with a meditative and somewhat melancholy expression, he uttered the following broken sentences: "After all it is endurable. . . . Men may live at any place and in any way. . . . The moment perhaps is not far remote— Themistocles! . . ." "The aide-de-camp who himself related this circumstance to me"— writes Las Cases—"observed that had the Emperor been successful (at Waterloo) these words would have passed away without leaving any impression on him, but that after the catastrophe and particularly after reading the celebrated letter to the Prince-Regent, he had been

[19] Marmont, II.

struck with the recollection of the bivouac of the Sambre; and Napoleon's manner, tone and expression had since so haunted his mind that he could never banish the circumstance from his memory." [20]

"Your Royal Highness . . . I come, like Themistocles, to throw myself upon the hospitality of the British people. I put myself under the protection of their laws, and beg Your Royal Highness, as the most powerful, the most persistent, and the most generous of my enemies to grant me this protection," writes Napoleon to the Prince Regent. [21]

Therefore, he knew, on the eve of Waterloo, what he would do at Rochefort.

This, however, is not so surprising. The amazing thing is that he knew it twenty-seven years before. About 1787, the seventeen-year-old Bonaparte started writing in his exercise books a story, in letter form, of an Austrian adventurer, Baron Neuhof, who in 1787 proclaimed himself king of Corsica under the name of Theodor I, was afterwards made a captive by the British, imprisoned in the Tower, and finally released by Walpole many years later. "How unjust is mankind. I wanted to make my

[20] *Memorial,* IV.
[21] Houssaye, *1815,* III.

people happy, and for one brief moment I succeeded; but fate was fickle to me, I am a prisoner, and surely you despise me," writes Theodor to Walpole, who replies: "You suffer, you are unfortunate: this is sufficient to give you a right to the compassion of the British people." "Dearly have I paid for my romantic and chivalrous opinion of you, *Messieurs les Anglais!*" It is as if at St. Helena Napoleon added the epilogue to the unfinished story of the Corsican pretender and captive of the British.[22]

These same exercise books contain excerpts from an old text-book of modern geography, "Géographie Moderne," by Abbé Lacroix, in which under British Dominions in Africa, Bonaparte wrote in, in his fine, compact, almost feminine handwriting of those days, four words:

> *Ste. Hélène petite isle*
> (St. Helena small island.)

Below—a blank page: the writing was begun but was left unfinished, as if his hand had been held back by someone.[23]

"Are you a fatalist?" "Yes, certainly. Like the Turks. I was always a fatalist. One must

[22] O'Meara.
[23] Masson, *Manuscrits.*

obey one's destiny." "One cannot miss one's destiny. One must be guided by one's star." [24]

Dying, he refuses to take medicine. "What is written in the heavens is written. . . . Our days are numbered," says he gazing at the sky.[25]

> Of heaven the prophetic sign is repeated on earth;
> Earth's prophetic sign is repeated in heaven. . . .

He would have understood the meaning of this ancient cuneiform Babylonian inscription.

Fatalism, the faith that the fate of man is determined by the stars, has been bequeathed to the modern East by Babylon, which in its turn received it from that immemorial, to us prehistoric, antiquity, which in Plato's myth is known as Atlantis, and in the Bible as the first human race before the flood. A starry chain links up Napoleon to that past. Of him, the last hero of the human race, the same may be said as of the first hero Gilgamish, that

> "A message he brought us from ages primordial."

"The Man of Destiny," "l'homme du destin." Thus was he named after Marengo by the Austrian Field-Marshal Melas. This name proved

[24] O'Meara, I.
[25] O'Meara.

to be one of those profound truisms which become common wisdom.

> He wears the grey coat of the soldier
> And a little cocked hat on his head. . . .

And the name: "The Man of Destiny."

Destiny to him is no abstract idea but a living being which influences his every thought, emotion, word or deed, governs every heart-throb. He lives within destiny as we live within space and time.

Immediately after the explosion of the infernal machine in the Rue Nikèze, the First Consul arrives at the Opera-house where he is greeted by two thousand spectators who know nothing of the attempt on his life. He bows to right and left in acknowledgment of their cheers with such a calm smile that no one guesses of his narrow escape from death a few moments before.[26] This is not fearlessness in our human sense nor a victory over fear, but the impossibility to experience it. He knows that Destiny shields him as a mother bearing her child in her arms. "For he shall give his angels charge over thee, to keep thee in all thy ways. They shall bear thee up in their hands, lest

[26] Abrantès, II

thou dash thy foot against a stone." This or something akin to this he knows, but does not as yet realize that it may be turned into a temptation of the devil: "If thou be the Son of God, cast thyself down from hence."

Angels of destiny or devils of chance bear him "for a season": his whole life then is one continuous miracle of soaring upward. "These were my happiest days," he said of the first campaign in Italy: "already I had the presentiment of what I might become. It was as if I were being lifted up into the air, and the world were disappearing beneath my feet!" [27]

This miracle of soaring lasted till the Russian campaign. "You are afraid I shall be killed in war?" he says just before it broke out. "During the period of conspiracies they used to try and scare me with the story that Georges [28] was was dogging my footsteps in order to assassinate me. The utmost he could do however was to murder my aide-de-camp. It was impossible to murder me at the time. Had I already fulfilled my destiny? I feel as if I am being driven towards an unknown goal. As soon as it is attained and there will no longer be any use for me, an atom will be sufficient to annihilate me; but

[27] Gourgaud, II.
[28] Georges Cadoudal, the Royalist conspirator.

until then, all human efforts whether in Paris or in the army will be powerless to prevail against me. But when my hour is struck, a touch of fever or a fall from my horse in the hunting field will kill me as surely as a cannon ball; our days are numbered in heaven." [29]

Another time, at Fontainebleau, also before the Russian campaign, Napoleon was engaged in a heated argument on church matters with his uncle, Cardinal Fesch, who entreated him at least not to rebel against God,—it was enough to be pitted against men. Napoleon listened in silence; then suddenly took him by the hand, led him to the door, opened it and stepped out on the balcony. It was a winter's day; the December sky showed pale blue between the black naked trees of the park. "Look at the sky. What do you see there?" asked Napoleon. "Nothing at all, Sire," replied Fesch. "Look well. Do you see anything?" "Nothing." "Well, then keep your own counsel and obey me. I see my Star: it guides me!" [30]

But Fesch never understood that Napoleon's great star was the Sun.

If there ever came a moment in his life when he suddenly became conscious that the hands

[29] Ségur, IV.
[30] Marmont, III. Ségur, IV.

which were bearing him upwards were failing
him, such a moment must be sought for at the
very pinnacle of his glory, at the highest point
attained in his soaring flight.

On the eve of Austerlitz, when already he
knew that to-morrow's sun "would rise
radiant," he started talking of ancient Greek
tragedy and said: "In our modern times, when
paganism is dead, tragedies need a new driving force. Politics, this is the mainspring which
must be substituted to ancient Fate." [31] To sub-
stitute fate by politics—the outcome of human
will, man needed to rebel against fate. No
sooner did Napoleon do this than his fall began: while he bowed in submission to Destiny
it raised him upward; when he rebelled against
it, he was hurled from the heights into the
abyss.

It would seem that he became conscious of
the downward bend in his fortunes just before
the beginning of the Russian campaign. "For
hours he would lie on the sofa plunged in
meditation; would suddenly start up with the
cry: 'Who is calling me?' and pace up and
down the room, murmuring to himself: 'No,
it's too soon, all is not ready yet . . . must be

[31] Ségur, II.

put off for another three years or so. . . .' [32]
But he knew that spurned by Destiny he would
postpone nothing.

"I failed in my expedition against the Russians. . . . Was I defeated by the efforts of the
Russians? No, my failure must be attributed
to pure accident, to absolute fatality. I did not
wish to give battle; neither did Alexander; but
being once in presence, circumstances urged us
on and fate accomplished the rest." He said this
at St. Helena, and "after a few moments of
silence and as if rousing himself from a
reverie" he begins to speak of trivial matters—
making out Bernadotte's treason as the chief
cause of his, Napoleon's, fall. [33]

Sleeping he has vision, and waking, is blind.

From Moscow to Leipzig the consciousness
of his coming fate grows ever clearer upon him.
"The circumstance which served to fill up the
measure of my distress, was that I beheld the
decisive hour gradually approach. The star
grew dim; I felt the reins slip from my hands,
and I yet could do nothing." [34] It is as if he were
in a lethargic sleep. He sees, hears and knows
all, but is powerless to rouse himself.

[32] Ségur, IV.
[33] *Memorial*, IV.
[34] *Memorial*, II.

"He was so utterly worn out and weary (at Leipzig) that when anyone approached him for orders, he would often lean back in a chair with his legs on the table whistling softly." [35] Perhaps after all, he was not "worn out," but preoccupied with other things and thoughts, weighed down by other burdens, hearkening to some other voices of Destiny. "Who calls me?" Only now, he was finishing the blank page headed seven and twenty years ago with the words: "St. Helena, small island."

"The spell that had hung over my miraculous career was broken. . . . Kind fortune no longer followed my footsteps and took pleasure in lavishing her smiles upon me; she was now succeeded by rigid fate, who took ample revenge for the few favours I obtained at this period, as it were by force. I marched through France (on the return from Elba) and arrived in the capital amidst the enthusiasm and universal acclamations of the people; but no sooner had I reached Paris, than by a sort of *magic* all around me retracted and grew cold." The power of magic had run out; the magnet attracted no longer. "Finally I triumphed even at Waterloo, and was immediately hurled into

[35] Stendhal.

255

the abyss. Yet I must confess that all these strokes of fate distressed me more than they surprised me. I felt the presentiment of an unfortunate result. Not that this in any way influenced my determinations and measures; but the foreboding certainty haunted my mind." [36]

"Nothing ever happened to me which I did not foresee." He foresees everything because he himself is the "magician" who conjures up the vision of his dream:

In the thick of dreams like a sorcerer's savage yelling
Sounded the thundering roar of the deep. . . .

"I ought to have died at Waterloo," says he at St. Helena, quite serenely, almost "cheerfully." "The worst of it is death never comes when it is sought after. Shells dropped all around me, in front and behind, but none touched me." [37] "A thousand shall fall at thy side and ten thousand at thy right hand, but it shall not come nigh thee." This invulnerability, once a blessing, now becomes a curse.

Clad in mighty armour, no danger thou reckest:
An invisible guardian is given thee, warrior!

[36] *Memorial,* IV.
[37] O'Meara, II.

Destiny

"I believe I owe it to *my star* that I have fallen into the hands of Hudson Lowe." [38] To such a fate had his "invisible guardian" led him.

"The heavy club which he alone could lift, now descended on his own head." [39] And it was as if he had known—remembered all along that this should be so; even, strange to say, seemed to want it should be so. Oh, certainly, it was an involuntary desire, as that of a man who gazing down into a precipice wants to hurl himself into it!

"When my great political chariot thunders past, woe to him who is caught under its wheels!" [40] He was caught under them himself. Then, did he understand at last?

> As in the embryo to the brain
> Articulation is complete, then turns the primal
> Mover with a smile of joy on such great work of
> Nature. . . .[41]

As he gazed upward at the starry *Cross* shining in the southern sky, did he realize at last what chariot was bearing him away and whither?

The victim is bound and crowned for the sacrifice. Did he understand that him, too, Des-

---

[38] O'Meara, I.
[39] Rémusat, I.

[40] Rémusat, III.
[41] Dante, *Purgat.* XXV.

tiny had crowned and bound as a victim? "The truth is, I never was master of my own action. I never was entirely myself. I never was truly my own master, but was always controlled by circumstances. Thus, at the commencement of my rise, during the Consulate, my sincere friends and warm partisans frequently asked me with the best intentions and as a guide for their own conduct, *what point was I driving at?* and I always answered that *I did not know.* They were surprised, probably dissatisfied, and yet I spoke the truth. . . . Subsequently, during the Empire . . . many faces seemed to put the same question to me; and I might still have given the same reply. In fact, I was not master of my action, because I was not fool enough to attempt to twist events into conformity with my system. On the contrary, I moulded my system according to the unforeseen succession of events. This often appeared like unsteadiness and inconsistency, and of these faults I was sometimes unjustly accused." [42]

"What I want, or whither I go, I know not." What a strange confession to be made by Napoleon, the most intelligent of men. He seems to repeat Goethe's immortal epitome of him:

[42] *Memorial,* IV.

"Napoleon who lived wholly for ideas, was nevertheless unable to grasp the nature of ideal motives." "This is beyond me," *"cela me passe!"* as he said after Staps' attempt on his life. Does not he resemble a man whom an irresistible force is leading as a blind man is led by the hand?

Here is another confession, stranger still: "I have no will-power. The greater the man, the less will-power he requires; he is entirely governed by events and circumstances." *"Plus on est grand, et moins on doit avoir de volonté."* Napoleon, the man possessed of infinite will-power, is will-less. He measures a hero's—his own—greatness by the renunciation of will. The alleged lord of the world is a veritable slave. "I tell you there is no greater slave than myself; my inexorable mistress is the nature of things!" Simply and in all humility he uses the expression the "nature of things" or "circumstances," so as not to use in vain the holy and awful name of Destiny.

Renunciation, humility, submissiveness, self-sacrifice—all these seemingly so alien are yet akin to him. "Not as I will, but as Thou wilt," he cannot say this as a son to a Father, for he knows not either Father or Son; yet it seems, as if the shadow of the Son fell upon him when he thus humbled himself before the unknown Deity with the veiled Face.

Spinoza has been called "A man intoxicated with God." Napoleon might well be called "a man intoxicated with Destiny."

"God gave it me; woe to him who touches it!" *"Dio me la donna, guia a che la toccera!"* he exclaimed as he laid upon his head the iron crown of the kings of Lombardy, in Milan. The name of God was invoked for the public, but surely to himself he pronounced it as: "Destiny." That is why his face wears an imprint of such sadness, or of that which is far deeper than any human sadness—of more than human thoughtfulness: it is the seal laid by Destiny on its votaries and on those who are sacrificed to Destiny.

"The first time I saw Bonaparte in the gloomy halls of the Tuileries palace I said to him: 'How sad it is here, General,' and he replied: 'Yes, sad as greatness,' " writes Roederer.[43] "Always there is a melancholy about him, even in his army orders and war bulletins." [44] Never, even in the thick of action, does an ever-present melancholy or pensiveness forsake him.

[43] Roederer.
[44] *Ibid.*

Destiny

"When in a confidential mood he confessed that in all conditions of life he was sadder beyond comparison than his comrades." [45] "I was not created for pleasure," [46] he would say in melancholy tones. "People bore me, honours pall, my heart is dried up, fame seems stale. At twenty-nine I have got to the end of everything." This he writes when at the height of success, during the campaign in Egypt. This already is *Weltschmerz*. It seems as if he were the first who did but open the door into this darkest of all nights, and the icy breath of these inter-planetary spaces rushed into the chamber . . .

> And when I die
> In this world I shall leave no brother.
> My weary soul is wrapped in cold and darkness.
> Like a fruit too early ripe, bereft of sap.
> In the storms of *destiny* my soul has withered
> Under the scorching sun of life. [47]

"Napoleon either smiles or laughs uproariously, but is never gay." [48] "Who once gazed down into the prophetic chasm of Trophonias will never laugh again," so runs the ancient saying.

[45] Rémusat, I.
[46] *Ibid.*

[47] M. Lermontov.
[48] Fain.

Napoleon

"Always alone, though in the midst of men, I go back home that I may give myself to my lonely dreams and to the waves of my melancholy. Whither, now, do my gloomy thoughts tend? Towards death," writes in his diary the seventeen-year-old Lieutenant Bonaparte, sitting in his poor little barrack room at Auxonne. And at the summit of his power the Emperor Napoleon wears on his breast a wallet with poison. The idea of suicide was always present with him, although he knew—"remembered" that he would never put an end to his life. This idea does not come to him from any outward misfortunes, but because he is weary of "the lethargic sleep" of life and longs to awaken at last, if only into death.

"Your restless spirit is always hankering for storms," Josephine says to him: "Strong in your desires, weak in happiness, it seems the only person you will never vanquish is yourself." [49]

Lord, why hast thou doomed Gilgamish to know no rest,
Hast withheld from him the gift of a peaceful heart?

Is the lament of the hero's mother.

Like Gilgamish, Napoleon is "the friend of sorrow."

[49] Ségur.

Destiny

From thee even life do I seek;
For him o'er plains I wander alone,
Follow his trail over oceans and rivers,
Impassible mountains I scale. . .
Broken I am by woes and misfortunes,
And blighted is now my beauteous image. . .

He too might have repeated this ancient
Babylonian prayer to the goddess Ishtar. Even
now the course of Gilgamish—Napoleon is not
yet run: ever-sorrowing and lamenting, as if
driven by some inexorable power he wanders
on and on and cannot stop, like Ahasuerus or
Cain. And his course is that of all the human
race.

He does not move of his own free will, but
is driven by some unknown force, as a stone is
thrown by an unknown hand. "I am a piece of
rock launched into space." (*"Je suis une parcelle
de rocher lancée dans l'espace."*) [50] He merely
follows on earth the course of the endless
parabola begun in those spaces from which he
descended, and his passage through our terrestrial sphere is like the flight of a meteor.

On the 8th of August, 1769, seven days before
Napoleon's birth, a comet appeared which was
signalled from the Paris Observatory by the astronomer Missiol. By the 20th September its

[50] *Memorial,* III.

marvellously brilliant tail was sixty degrees long and gradually approached the sun until it disappeared completely in its rays as if the comet itself had become the sun—the great star of Napoleon.

In the beginning of February, 1821, three months before Napoleon's death, a comet again appeared above St. Helena. "It was observed in Paris on the 11th January," writes the astronomer Faye. "In February it became visible to the naked eye and its tail attained a length of seven degrees. It was observed throughout the whole of Europe, and between April 21st to May 5th also in Valparaiso." Thus, it was visible in both hemispheres, across the whole Atlantic—the last stage of Napoleon's earthly course.

"His servants affirm having seen a comet in the east," writes Dr. Antommarchi in his diary under 2nd of April, 1821. "I went into his room and found him greatly perturbed by the news. 'A comet,' he exclaimed with emotion: 'A comet was the sign which predicted the death of Cæsar . . . and now prophesies my own. . . .' " [51] "On the 5th of May (day of Napoleon's death), writes the same astronomer,

[51] Antommarchi, II.

Faye, the comet could be observed from St. Helena through a telescope, slowly receding from the earth and disappearing into space." [52]

"Poor fellow! How I pity him," thus wrote in 1791 an obscure lieutenant of artillery, Bonaparte, of a man of genius—himself. "He will become an object of wonder and envy to his fellow-men and *the most miserable of them all, le plus misérable de tous.* . . . Men of genius are like meteors: they must shine and consume themselves that they may lighten the darkness of their age." [53]

Consummation, death, sacrifice—such is his destiny—this he knew at the beginning of his life, and learnt still better at the end, on St. Helena beneath the constellation of the Cross: "Jesus Christ would not have been the Son of God, if He hadn't died upon the Cross." Yet this knowledge is obscured from him, as the sun to the blind: unable to see the light of the sun: they only feel its warmth,—so it is with him.

On the island of Gorgon he offered a sacrifice to Moloch, the Sun-god; here on St. Helena he is himself offered up in sacrifice—to whom —he knows not, and thinks it is to Destiny.

His star faded away in the rays of the sun.

[52] Antommarchi, Nobe. D. Lacroix.
[53] Masson, *Manuscrits.*

Napoleon

The nature of that sun is also unknown to him, and again he calls it—Destiny.

The ancients used the name of Destiny for what we call "the laws of nature," or "necessity." The essence of both is death, the annihilation of personality, for the law of nature is as impersonal as is Destiny. The choice lay between life or death, the meek yoke of the Son or the iron yoke of Destiny. We chose the latter, and are now fallen as its victims, as fell Napoleon, our last hero, the greatest and "the most miserable" of us all.

His prophetic dream is like that of Jacob: "And Jacob was left alone; and there wrestled a man with him until the breaking of the day. And when he saw that he prevailed not against him . . . he said: Let me go for the day breaketh. And he said, I will not let thee go, except thou bless me." Jacob wrestles with God, and Napoleon—with the Son of God. Napoleon, the Man, wrestles with Him as does all mankind which has denied Christ.

"Is Christianity a success?" is an impious question. It should be asked: is our European Christian humanity a success? Will it find its salvation in and with Christ, or, having denied Him perish like a second Atlantis? This is the

question put to us by "the man from Atlantis"—
Napoleon.

He is the last hero of the West. "We have
come to the setting sun, and having beheld the
glow of eventide, we praise God, Father, Son
and Holy Spirit!" [54] thus sung the early Christians. We no longer praise anyone as we gaze
at the evening glow in the West, surrounding
our last hero with a halo of glory. The light of
eventide is behind him; that is why his face
to us is so dark and inscrutable and becoming
ever darker and stranger in the ever waning
light. Yet not for nothing, perhaps, it is turned
towards the East; the first rays of the rising sun
of the Son will illumine it, and we shall then
see and recognize him.

Yea, only when men acknowledge and recognize the Son of Man, then, and only then will
the truth of Napoleon, the Man, be revealed
to them.

[54] Early Christian hymn, sung in the Eastern Church.

DATE DUE